THE OFFICIAL BETTER BRIDGE SERIES

BRIDGE BASICS 1

An Introduction

Audrey Grant

Published by
Baron Barclay Bridge Supplies

Bridge Basics 1: An Introduction
Copyright © 2004 Audrey Grant's Better Bridge Inc.

If you'd like to contact the author, see page 205.

Baron Barclay Bridge Supplies
3600 Chamberlain Lane, Suite 230
Louisville, KY 40241
U.S. and Canada: 1-800-274-2221
Worldwide: 502-426-0410
FAX: 502-426-2044

www.baronbarclay.com

ISBN 0-939460-11-4

Illustrations by Kelvin Smith
Design and composition by John Reinhardt Book Design

Printed in the United States of America

Contents

Contents

Contents

The Bridge Basics Series

The Improving Your Judgment Series

... more to come

Introduction

Bridge has captivated players for many years. It has evolved and changed but the fascination of the game and its appeal to players of all ages is still strong. There have always been different approaches and bidding styles. The **BRIDGE BASICS SERIES** uses Audrey Grant Standard, which is a modern approach, played in most games online, at tournaments, in golf clubs, on board ships, and among friends playing at home. The advisory committee for this system consists of the best players in the world.

BRIDGE BASICS I — AN INTRODUCTION provides a well-balanced overview of bidding, play and defense. The thirty-two carefully prepared deals give you the chance to practice what you've learned. This advances your skill playing the cards and puts the bidding in a meaningful context.

Bridge provides the opportunity for adventure and mental fitness—a wonderful combination. We look forward to bringing you the best bridge information the world has to offer.

All the best,

Audrey Grant
www.AudreyGrant.com

Acknowledgments

To my husband, *David Lindop*, a world-class player who works hand-in-hand with me to produce the bridge books.

To *Jason Grant-Lindop* and *Joanna Grant* for their support and involvement in the many aspects of Better Bridge.

To the Better Bridge Advisory Committee:

- *Bob Hamman* — World Champion, world's top-ranked male player
- *Petra Hamman* — World Champion, bridge teacher
- *Shawn Quinn* — World Champion, world's top-ranked female player
- *Fred Gitelman* — Founder of Bridge Base Inc., gold medallist
- *Henry Francis* — Editor of the Official Encyclopedia of Bridge
- *Jerry Helms* — Professional bridge teacher and player

To the bridge teachers. Your dedication, skill, and professionalism has made me proud to be counted among you.

To the students of the game—thank you for sharing your ideas and your enthusiasm.

The pleasures Ivan Ilyich derived from his work were those of pride; the pleasures he derived from society those of vanity; but it was genuine pleasure that he derived from playing whist.

—LEO TOLSTOY, THE DEATH OF IVAN ILYICH

The Basics

The Players

Bridge is a game played with four people. The players sit facing each other around a table and are often referred to by the four points on a compass: North, South, East, and West. The players sitting opposite one another form a *partnership*: North and South play against East and West. The partnerships and initial *dealer* can be pre-arranged or chosen through a draw of the cards (see Appendix 1).

```
        NORTH


WEST  ←  ✛  →  EAST


        SOUTH
```

The Deck

A regular *deck* of fifty-two cards is used. There are four *suits*: spades (♠), hearts (♥), diamonds (♦), and clubs (♣) and thirteen cards in each suit. The ace is the highest card, then the king, queen, jack, ten...down to the two.

The Deal

The cards are dealt face-down, one at a time, clockwise, starting with the player to the dealer's left. At the end of the deal, each player has thirteen cards which are referred to as a bridge *hand*. After the cards

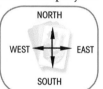

have been dealt, each player picks up the hand and sorts it into suits. It's easiest to view a hand if you alternate the red and black suits and arrange the cards in each suit with the highest cards on the left.

Trick-taking

Bridge is a trick-taking game. A *trick* consists of four cards, one from each player in turn, clockwise around the table. One player *leads* a card by putting it face up on the table[1]. The other players have to *follow suit* by playing a card of the same suit as the one led. The play to a trick looks like this:

West leads the ♥K. North plays the ♥6 and East the ♥2. South wins the trick with the ♥A, the highest card in the suit. South now leads to the next trick.

If a player can't follow suit, a card from another suit is played. This is called *discarding*. The highest card in the suit led wins the trick and the player winning the trick leads to the next trick.

West leads the ♣Q. North plays the ♣A and East discards the ♦4. East has no clubs remaining. South follows suit with the ♣5.

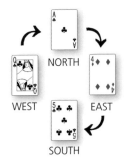

Play continues until thirteen tricks have been played.

---

[1] In some forms of the game, the opening lead is made face down (see Appendix 1).

Recording Tricks

After a trick has been won, there are two ways to record the result. In *rubber bridge*, a player from the winning side collects the four cards, turns them face-down and stacks the cards in a neat pile at the edge of the table. One player from each side collects the tricks won by the partnership. As each trick is collected, it's offset slightly from previous tricks, making it easy to count the tricks won. The table might look like this:

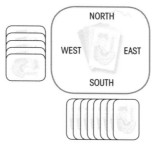

Another way to record tricks is *duplicate* style. Each card played to a trick is kept in front of the player. After all four cards have been played, the cards are turned face down. If the trick is won, the card is placed vertically; if it is lost it is placed horizontally. Since bridge is a partnership game, if one player on a team wins the trick both players put the card in the winning, vertical position. The cards are placed along the edge of the table. Here's an example:

Trick one [won]

Trick two [lost]

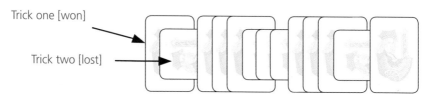

If these are the cards in front of you at the end of the deal, your side has won eight tricks, the cards placed vertically, and has lost five tricks, the cards placed horizontally. The advantage is that at the end of the deal, you could pick the cards up and look at the hand again.

Taking Tricks in a Trump Suit

A bridge deal can be played in either *notrump* or a *trump* suit. In notrump, the highest card played in the suit led wins the trick. In a trump suit, one suit is trumps. If a player can't follow suit, a trump can be played. This is called *trumping* or *ruffing*.

A trump beats any card in another suit. If more than one player is unable to follow suit to the lead, the highest trump played wins the trick.

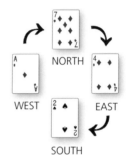

Suppose spades are trumps. West leads the ♦A, North follows suit with the ♦7 and East with the ♦4. South, unable to follow suit in diamonds, plays the ♠2, which wins the trick.

Playing a trump when you can't follow suit is optional. You can discard instead of trumping. For example, if East held no diamonds, East could discard another suit instead of trumping because partner's ♦A is winning the trick. The trump suit can be led at any time. The highest trump played to the trick wins.

Choosing a Trump Suit

Whist

In whist, a predecessor of bridge, the last card dealt was turned face up and that suit became trumps. The dealer then picked up the card and the deal was played out. The game involved an element of luck because the partnership with the majority of trump cards had an advantage in the play.

Auction Bridge

Selecting the trump suit is an important part of the game. Whist evolved into *auction bridge*. The choice of the trump suit was no longer left to chance. Instead, the players had an *auction* for the privilege of naming the trump suit.

Starting with the dealer and moving clockwise around the table, each player has a chance to *call*. A call is a *bid* to suggest a trump suit or notrump, or a *pass*[2]. If no one is willing to bid and all four players pass, a new deal is started. Otherwise, once a player *opens the bidding*, the auction continues until three players, in succession, pass.

The Language of Bidding

A bid consists of two parts, a *level* and a *strain*. The level is the number of tricks the partnership is willing to try to take beyond an initial six tricks, called *book*. So, a bid at the *one level* is a commitment to take at least seven tricks, six plus one. To start the bidding, therefore, the partnership has to be willing to take the majority of the tricks. The highest bid is seven, a commitment to take all thirteen tricks, six plus seven.

The strain is the suggested trump suit or the suggestion to play in notrump. For example:

"One Heart" (1♥ or 1H)—A commitment to take at least seven tricks (six plus one) with hearts as trumps.

"Two Diamonds" (2♦ or 2D)—A commitment to take at least eight tricks (six plus two) with diamonds as trumps.

"Three Notrump" (3NT)—A commitment to take at least nine tricks (six plus three) with no trump suit.

The partnership willing to try to take more tricks during the play wins the auction.

---

[2] Two additional calls, the *double* and *redouble* are discussed in the next book in this series, COMPETITIVE BIDDING.

The Bidding Ladder

The bidding can result in a tie. One partnership might be willing to take seven tricks with hearts as trumps; the other side might be willing to take seven tricks with spades as trumps. To break ties, the suits are *ranked* in alphabetical order with clubs as the lowest ranking suit, then diamonds, hearts, and spades. Notrump is ranked higher than any suit.

Each bid must be higher than the one before.

For example, suppose the dealer bids 1♥, committing to seven tricks with hearts as the trump suit. The auction moves clockwise to the opponent on the dealer's left. To suggest spades as the trump suit, that player could bid, or *overcall*, 1♠, since spades are higher ranking than hearts. To suggest diamonds as the trump suit, the player would have to overcall 2♦, going up a level on the Bidding Ladder and committing to eight tricks.

The auction progresses up the Bidding Ladder until there are three passes in a row, with no one willing to bid any higher.

On some deals only one side *competes* during the bidding conversation. On other deals both sides compete for the privilege of naming trumps. This book focuses on bidding without competition, where only one side is bidding[3].

	7NT
7-Level	7♠
(13 Tricks)	7♥
	7♦
	7♣
	6NT
6-Level	6♠
(12 Tricks)	6♥
	6♦
	6♣
	5NT
5-Level	5♠
(11 Tricks)	5♥
	5♦
	5♣
	4NT
4-Level	4♠
(10 Tricks)	4♥
	4♦
	4♣
	3NT
3-Level	3♠
(9 Tricks)	3♥
	3♦
	3♣
	2NT
2-Level	2♠
(8 Tricks)	2♥
	2♦
	2♣
	1NT
1-Level	1♠
(7 Tricks)	1♥
	1♦
	1♣

BIDDING LADDER

[3] Sample Deal 3 illustrates an example of an overcall.

The Key to Selecting a Trump Suit

The partnership is ideally searching for an eight-card or longer combined *trump fit*. If an eight-card fit cannot be found, the partnership will usually settle in a notrump contract. Much of the bidding discussion for the remainder of this book will focus on how the partnership communicates through the auction to uncover a suitable trump fit.

Declarer and Dummy

Auction bridge introduced another change from whist. This was the way the deal was played out after the auction[4].

The player who first names, or declares, the strain for the side which wins the auction is called the *declarer*. The hand of declarer's partner is referred to as the *dummy*.

The player to the left of declarer makes the *opening lead* to the first trick. The dummy hand is then placed face up on the table in four columns of suits facing declarer, with the highest cards closest to the edge of the table. If there is a trump suit, it is placed to dummy's right, declarer's left. Declarer makes the decision about the cards to be played to a trick from both partnership hands.

DUMMY ➡

Trump suit ➡
in a trump contract

Opening lead ➡

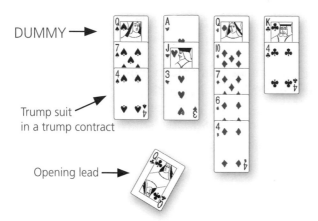

---

[4] This concept was originally introduced in dummy whist, a variation of whist that was played before auction bridge.

Once the dummy is placed face up on the table, playing rubber bridge, declarer selects the card to be played from the dummy and puts it in the middle of the table. In duplicate bridge, declarer names the card to be played from dummy and declarer's partner places it close to the edge of the table. Then, the opponent to declarer's right plays a card and, finally, declarer plays a card to complete the first trick. The hand winning the first trick leads to the second trick, and play continues until all thirteen tricks have been played.

The declarer's side will become the *offense*, with the declarer trying to make the contract during the play. The other side becomes the *defense*, trying to prevent declarer from taking the required number of tricks.

Contract Bridge

A problem with auction bridge was that the play was not always exciting. To win the auction it was only necessary to outbid the other partnership. If the other side was unwilling to compete, the auction could be won at the one level and declarer was only committed to take seven tricks.

To increase the challenge, bonuses were awarded if the partnership was willing to commit, or *contract*, to take a specified number of tricks and was then able to fulfill, or *make*, the contract during the play. Auction bridge evolved into *contract bridge*, the form of the game today.

This makes the auction and play much more challenging. Even if both sides aren't competing for the privilege of naming the trump suit, one partnership may continue bidding until a bonus level contract is reached. Since the bidding usually goes higher than in auction bridge, there is more chance for the defenders to *defeat*, or *set*, the contract and receive a bonus.

The Bidding Ladder and the Bonus Levels

There are three bonus levels: grand slam; small slam; and game.

Slam Bonuses

A bonus is awarded if the partnership bids and makes a *grand slam* contract, all thirteen tricks, or a *small slam*, twelve tricks. This doesn't happen that often.

Game Bonuses

The level to which the partnership has to bid to get a *game* bonus depends on the strain:

```
┌─────────────────────────────────────────┐
│          GAME BONUS LEVELS               │
│                                          │
│  Five Diamonds (5♦)  }                   │
│  Five Clubs (5♣)     } At least eleven tricks│
│                                          │
│  Four Spades (4♠)    }                   │
│  Four Hearts (4♥)    } At least ten tricks│
│                                          │
│  Three Notrump (3NT)  At least nine tricks│
└─────────────────────────────────────────┘
```

Because they require fewer tricks for a game bonus, hearts and spades are referred to as the *major suits*. Clubs and diamonds are the *minor suits*.

Partscore

A contract that does not reach a game or slam bonus level is called a *partscore*, or a *part game*.

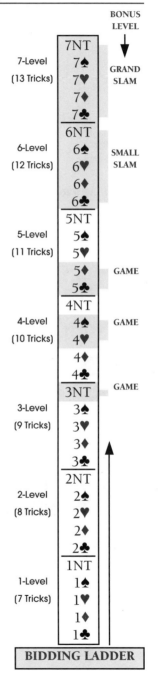

		BONUS LEVEL
	7NT	
7-Level	7♠	GRAND SLAM
(13 Tricks)	7♥	
	7♦	
	7♣	
	6NT	
6-Level	6♠	SMALL SLAM
(12 Tricks)	6♥	
	6♦	
	6♣	
	5NT	
5-Level	5♠	
(11 Tricks)	5♥	
	5♦	GAME
	5♣	
	4NT	
4-Level	4♠	GAME
(10 Tricks)	4♥	
	4♦	
	4♣	
	3NT	GAME
3-Level	3♠	
(9 Tricks)	3♥	
	3♦	
	3♣	
	2NT	
2-Level	2♠	
(8 Tricks)	2♥	
	2♦	
	2♣	
	1NT	
1-Level	1♠	
(7 Tricks)	1♥	
	1♦	
	1♣	

BIDDING LADDER

Scoring

The game can be scored in different ways. A more detailed look at scoring can be found in Appendix 2.

Overtricks and Undertricks

Tricks taken beyond those needed to make the contract are *overtricks*. Tricks by which declarer falls short of making the contract are called *undertricks*.

Hand Valuation

To decide whether you can afford to bid you need some estimate of the trick-taking potential of the hand. This is usually done by assigning *valuation points* to useful features of the hand.

The *high cards* in a hand—aces, kings, queens, and jacks—are valuable for taking tricks. Since an ace is more valuable than a king and so on, these cards are assigned valuation points, called *high-card points* (*HCPs*):

HIGH CARD POINTS (HCPs)	
Ace	4 points
King	3 points
Queen	2 points
Jack	1 point

There are 40 high-card points in the deck, 10 in each suit.

The *distribution*, or *shape*, of the hand—the number of cards in each suit—also plays a part. A long suit is useful as a potential trump suit and as a source of tricks. There are different ways to value distribution but the most common in today's game is to assign a valuation point, called a *length point*, for each card beyond four in a suit:

LENGTH POINTS	
5-card suit	1 point
6-card suit	2 points
7-card suit	3 points
8-card suit	4 points

The high-card points (HCPs) are added to the length points to provide an initial estimate of the value of the hand – the *point count* or *strength*. For example:

	HIGH-CARD POINTS (HCPS)	LENGTH POINTS
♠ Q 7 4	2	
♥ A J 3	(4 + 1) = 5	
♦ Q 10 7 6 4	2	1
♣ K 4	3	
	12	1

This hand is worth 13 valuation points: 12 high-card points and 1 length point for the fifth diamond.

Relating Valuation Points to Trick-Taking Potential

A partnership with no valuation points in the *combined hands* would probably take no tricks. A partnership holding all the points might be expected to take all the tricks. Experience has shown the approximate relationship between valuation points and the bonus levels. This is illustrated on the Bidding Ladder.

The games are the most frequent bonus levels. To take nine tricks in notrump requires about 25 combined points[5]; a game in spades or hearts requires about 26 points; and a game in diamonds or clubs about 29 points.

A First Look at Opening the Bidding

To start the auction, the following guidelines can be used:

- With fewer than 13 points, pass;
- With 13 or more points, open the bidding.

For now, start with the *longest suit*, not the strongest, when suggesting a trump suit. With two equal length suits, open the higher-ranking. The choice of opening bid is discussed in more detail in the upcoming chapters[6].

[5] Some textbooks suggest a more conservative approach requiring 26 or more points for a game in notrump.

[6] Appendix 3 has the words to the BIDDING SONG. A different verse applies to each chapter in the book.

BONUS LEVEL (COMBINED VALUATION PTS.)

Level	Bid	Bonus
	7NT	
7-Level	7♠	GRAND SLAM 37+
(13 Tricks)	7♥	
	7♦	
	7♣	
	6NT	
6-Level	6♠	SMALL SLAM 33+
(12 Tricks)	6♥	
	6♦	
	6♣	
	5NT	
5-Level	5♠	
(11 Tricks)	5♥	
	5♦	GAME 29+ PTS.
	5♣	
	4NT	
4-Level	4♠	GAME 26+ PTS.
(10 Tricks)	4♥	
	4♦	
	4♣	
	3NT	GAME 25+ PTS.
3-Level	3♠	
(9 Tricks)	3♥	
	3♦	
	3♣	
	2NT	
2-Level	2♠	
(8 Tricks)	2♥	
	2♦	
	2♣	
	1NT	
1-Level	1♠	
(7 Tricks)	1♥	
	1♦	
	1♣	

BIDDING LADDER

A First Look at Responding

The partner of the opening bidder is called the *responder*. The response depends on the opening bid. The general idea is that responder bids to compete if the opponents are also bidding, or to improve the contract.

Recording a Complete Deal

For the purpose of representing a deal in a newspaper or a book, the following format is used:

The four suits are displayed with the highest-ranking, spades, at

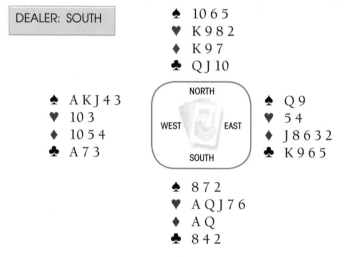

DEALER: SOUTH

♠ 10 6 5
♥ K 9 8 2
♦ K 9 7
♣ Q J 10

NORTH
WEST   EAST
SOUTH

♠ A K J 4 3
♥ 10 3
♦ 10 5 4
♣ A 7 3

♠ Q 9
♥ 5 4
♦ J 8 6 3 2
♣ K 9 6 5

♠ 8 7 2
♥ A Q J 7 6
♦ A Q
♣ 8 4 2

the top and the lowest-ranking, clubs, at the bottom. "A" represents the ace, "K" the king, "Q" the queen, and "J" the jack.

South is indicated as the dealer. The auction is represented in this manner:

WEST	NORTH	EAST	SOUTH
			1♥
1♠	2♥	PASS	PASS
PASS			

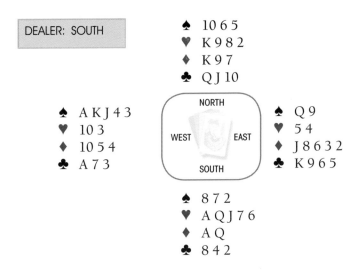

DEALER: SOUTH

NORTH
♠ 10 6 5
♥ K 9 8 2
♦ K 9 7
♣ Q J 10

WEST
♠ A K J 4 3
♥ 10 3
♦ 10 5 4
♣ A 7 3

EAST
♠ Q 9
♥ 5 4
♦ J 8 6 3 2
♣ K 9 6 5

SOUTH
♠ 8 7 2
♥ A Q J 7 6
♦ A Q
♣ 8 4 2

In this auction, South is the dealer and opens the bidding 1♥, suggesting hearts as the trump suit. West bids, overcalls, 1♠. North responds 2♥ and East, South, and West all pass. The contract is 2♥. South, who first suggested hearts as the trump suit, is the declarer and will try to take eight tricks. West, to declarer's left, will make the opening lead and North will then put the hand face up on the table as the dummy.

DECLARER'S PLAN—THE ABC'S

You're the declarer. The opponent to your left makes the opening lead and partner puts down the dummy. Before choosing the first card to play from dummy, plan how you are going to take enough tricks to make the contract. There are three suggested stages—A, B, and C—in making a plan:

DECLARER'S PLAN — THE ABC'S

Assess the Situation
Browse Declarer's Checklist to Develop Extra Tricks
Consider the Order

Assess the Situation

This stage can be divided into three steps:

- Goal
- Sure Tricks
- Extra Tricks Needed

1) **Goal**. Start by considering the number of tricks required to make the contract. In 1NT, for example, you need to take seven tricks; in 2♥ you need to take eight tricks.

2) **Sure Tricks**[7]. Count the *sure tricks*. Sure tricks or, *winners*, are those that can be taken without giving up the lead. An ace is a sure trick; an ace and a king in the same suit are two sure tricks.

3) **Extra Tricks Needed**. Compare the number of tricks you need to the number of sure tricks you have. If you have the number of tricks you need, move to the third stage; otherwise, go to the second stage.

For example, suppose you are declarer in a 3NT contract and count seven tricks that can be taken right away. The assessment of the situation would look like this:

- Goal   9 ◄— You need nine tricks to make 3NT.
- Sure Tricks   7 ◄— You have seven sure tricks.
- Extra Tricks Needed   2 ◄— The difference is two.

Browse Declarer's Checklist to Develop Extra Tricks

There are several techniques used to develop, or *establish*, extra tricks when you don't have enough to make the contract. These are discussed in the upcoming chapters.

---

[7] In trump contracts, *losers* are sometimes counted instead of winners. This is discussed in DE-CLARER PLAY.

Consider the Order

When developing and taking tricks, the order in which the tricks are played is often very important. For now, here are two considerations when you have the tricks you need:

1) **Draw trumps**. In a trump contract, an important consideration is whether to *draw the opponents' trumps* by playing the trump suit until the defenders have none left. If you have the tricks you need, start by drawing trumps. Now the opponents will not be able to use their trumps to ruff any of your winners in another suit.

2) **Take the tricks**. The opponents are trying to take enough tricks to defeat the contract. If you have the tricks you need, take the tricks and run. Make the contract before anything goes wrong. Extra tricks aren't as important as fulfilling the contract.

Defense – Choosing a Card

The partnership on defense tries to defeat the contract. Like declarer, the defenders should make a plan, but this is more challenging because they can't see each other's cards and can't even see the dummy until after the opening lead is made. Instead, the defenders usually follow some general guidelines until they can clearly see a way of defeating the contract.

The Opening Lead — The First Card Played

There are two steps to selecting the opening lead:

- Choose the suit to lead.
- Choose the specific card within that suit.

The principles for defending against notrump contracts differ from those for defending against a suit (trump) contract, so the choice of opening lead will depend on the contract.

OPENING LEAD AGAINST NOTRUMP

When defending against a notrump contract, the partnership usually wants to try to develop winners in its longest combined suit. Because there is no trump suit, declarer can't stop the defenders from taking their established winners once they gain the lead. If partner bid a suit during the auction, lead that suit. Otherwise, the guideline for choosing the suit is:

- Choose the longest suit.
- With a choice among suits of equal length, choose the strongest suit.

The defenders can exchange information through the card that is led. When the suit has a *sequence*, three or more touching cards, that is headed by an *honor*, the top of the touching high cards is led. An honor is one of the top five cards in the suit—the ace, king, queen, jack, or ten. So, if partner leads the ♣Q, you know partner doesn't have the next higher-ranking card, the ♣K, but does hold the next lower-ranking card, the ♠J and likely the ♠10 as well[8].

If the longest suit doesn't have a sequence, the guideline is to pick a low card. From the days of whist, the popular guideline has been: lead fourth highest from the longest and strongest suit. The *fourth highest* is the fourth down from the top.

So, the guideline for choosing the card is:

- Lead the top of touching high cards from a three-card or longer sequence.
- Lead the fourth highest card from the longest and strongest suit.

---

[8] The top of a broken sequence is also led against a notrump contract: A-K-J-4-3, K-Q-10-7. The top of an interior sequence can also be led: A-J-10-3, K-10-9-5-4.

Consider the following hands on opening lead against a 1NT contract:

♠ K Q J 5 3 ♥ 7 5 4 ♦ A K 6 ♣ 4 2	The ♦A and ♦K could be taken right away but that is only two tricks. The guideline is to start with the longest suit, spades. Since the suit has a three-card sequence, the top of the touching cards, the ♠K, would be the opening lead.
♠ 8 4 ♥ K 9 7 5 2 ♦ Q 7 4 3 2 ♣ 9	With two equally long suits, the stronger, hearts, is chosen. Since there is no honor sequence, a low card is led, the ♥5, fourth highest.

OPENING LEAD AGAINST A SUIT CONTRACT

When there is a trump suit, the strategy changes. Leading the longest suit has less appeal. Even if winners can be established in the suit, declarer's trump suit can prevent the defenders from taking them. When choosing the suit, it is preferable to pick one with two or more touching cards headed by an honor. On occasion, a short suit can be led with the hope of trumping declarer's winners in the suit.

When choosing the card:

- Lead the top of two or more touching high cards.
- Lead the top of a two-card suit, if leading a short suit.
- Otherwise, lead low[9], fourth highest from a four-card or longer suit.

Consider the following hands on lead against a 2♥ contract:

♠ A 8 3 ♥ 4 ♦ Q J 10 4 ♣ K 8 7 4 2	Although the club suit is longer, the diamond suit would likely be chosen instead because of the honor sequence. With touching high cards, the top card, ♦Q, would be led.

[9] Against a suit contract, a low card is not usually led if the suit has the ace. Instead, the ace is preferred, or another suit.

♠ 8 4 3 2
♥ 7 5 2
♦ Q 7 4 3 2
♣ 9

The lead of the ♣9 might be chosen, hoping to make use of one of the low trumps to ruff declarer's winners in the club suit.

Leading to Subsequent Tricks

Unless there is clearly a better choice, a useful guideline is to return the suit led by partner. The partnership wants to work together to develop tricks.

Second Hand Play

When the first card to a trick is led by declarer or from dummy and you are next to play, you are referred to as *second hand*. Here are two useful guidelines:

- If a low card is led, you generally play a low card, second hand low. Your partner will be playing last to the trick and will be better placed to know what to do.
- If an honor is led, another guideline is to cover an honor with an honor. If the ♠Q is led from dummy, for example, and you hold the ♠K, you can play it. If declarer wins the ♠A, you have used up two of their honors for one of yours.

Third Hand Play

If partner leads to a trick, you are *third hand*, playing the third card to the trick. The general guidelines are:

- If partner's card is winning, or likely to win, the trick, play low.
- Otherwise, play third hand high, attempting to win the trick.

Applying the Guidelines

There are many strategies for play and defense. As you gain experience, you'll be able to recognize the exceptions to the guidelines.

SUMMARY

The Auction

- Beginning with the dealer and continuing clockwise around the table, each player can make a bid or pass.
- A bid suggests a level and a strain.
- To open the bidding, a player should have about 13 or more valuation points.
- After the bidding has been opened, the auction continues until three players, in succession, pass.
- The last bid becomes the contract.
- The player who first suggested the strain for the side that wins the auction becomes the declarer. The other partnership defends.

The Play

- The defender to declarer's left makes the opening lead.
- Declarer's partner puts down the dummy in four columns, one for each suit. If there is a trump suit it goes on dummy's right.
- A card is played by each player in turn, clockwise around the table. The four cards constitute a trick.
- Each player has to follow suit, if possible. Otherwise, the player can discard or trump.
- Declarer selects the card to be played from the dummy and the card to be played from declarer's hand.
- The highest card in the suit led, or the highest trump played, wins the trick.
- The hand that wins the trick leads to the next trick.
- Play continues until all thirteen tricks have been played.

Declarer's Plan—The ABCs

Assess the Situation
- Goal
- Sure Tricks
- Extra Tricks Needed

Browse Declarer's Checklist if Extra Tricks are Required (see Chapter 2)

Consider the Order

If you have the tricks you need:
- Draw trumps first in a suit contract.
- Take the tricks and run

Defense

OPENING LEAD AGAINST A NOTRUMP CONTRACT:

Choose the suit:
- If partner has bid, lead that suit.
- Otherwise, lead the longest suit.
- With a choice of suits choose the strongest.

Choose the card:
- Lead the top of a sequence.
- Lead the fourth highest card with no sequence.

OPENING LEAD AGAINST A SUIT CONTRACT:

Choose the suit:
- If partner has bid, lead that suit.
- A suit with a strong sequence.
- A short suit.

Choose the card:
- Lead the top of touching cards.
- Lead the top of a two-card suit.
- Lead the fourth highest card.

ADDITIONAL TIPS:
- Second hand generally plays low.
- Third hand generally plays high.
- Return partner's lead.

Quiz – Part I

What number best describes each of the following:
  a) The cards in the deck used in a bridge game?
  b) The suits in a deck?
  c) The cards in each suit?
  d) The players in a bridge game?
  e) The players in a partnership?
  f) The cards in a player's hand at the beginning of a deal?
  g) The cards played to a trick?
  h) The tricks available in a bridge deal?

Suppose the auction proceeds as follows:

WEST	NORTH	EAST	SOUTH
	PASS	1♠	2♣
2♠	PASS	PASS	PASS

  i) Who is the dealer?
  j) What was the dealer's first call?
  k) Who is the opening bidder?
  l) What is the minimum number of valuation points East holds?
  m) Which player has made an overcall?
  n) Why has South bid at the two level?
  o) Who is the responder to the opening bidder?
  p) What bid did responder make?
  q) Who is the partner of the overcaller?
  r) What call did North make?
  s) Which side won the auction?
  t) What is the trump suit?
  u) Who will be the declarer?
  v) Who will make the opening lead?
  w) Which hand will be put down as the dummy?
  x) How many tricks does declarer have to take?
  y) How many tricks do the defenders have to take to defeat declarer?

Answers to Quiz – Part I

a) **Fifty-two**. All the cards in the deck except jokers are used.

b) **Four**. The four suits are clubs, diamonds, hearts, and spades.

c) **Thirteen**. The cards in each suit go from the ace to the two.

d) **Four**. The four players are typically equated with the points of a compass, North, South, East and West.

e) **Two**. North and South are partners; East and West are partners.

f) **Thirteen**. Each player is dealt 13 of the 52 cards.

g) **Four**. One card is contributed by each player.

h) **Thirteen**. This is the same as the number of cards in a hand.

i) **North**. The dealer can pass or bid.

j) **Pass**. North did not have enough to open the bidding.

k) **East**. East opened the auction with a 1♠ bid.

l) **13**. 13 or more valuation points are typically needed to open the auction at the one level.

m) **South**. South overcalled the 1♠ bid with a bid of 2♣.

n) **Clubs are lower-ranking than spades**. To suggest clubs as the trump suit, South has to move up a level on the Bidding Ladder.

o) **West**. Responder is the partner of the opening bidder.

p) **2♠**. West agreed with East's suggestion of spades as trumps.

q) **North**. North is the partner of the overcaller.

r) **Pass**. North did not wish to bid any higher.

s) **East-West**. The East-West partnership outbid North-South for the right to name the trump suit.

t) **Spades**. East and West have agreed on spades as trumps.

u) **East**. East first suggested spades for the partnership that won the auction.

v) **South**. South is the defender to declarer's left.

w) **West**. West is declarer's partner and will place the dummy hand face up on the table after the opening lead is made.

x) **Eight**. The contract is 2♠ which requires 8 (6 + 2) tricks.

y) **Six**. There are only thirteen tricks available. If North-South take six or more tricks, declarer won't make the contract.

Quiz – Part II

Determine the valuation points in each of the following hands. If you are the dealer, what is your call?

a) ♠ A 7 3
♥ K 8 4
♦ Q 10 7 5
♣ J 7 2

VALUATION: _____
CALL: _____

b) ♠ A Q J 4
♥ 9
♦ A K 8 3 2
♣ K 10 5

VALUATION: ___
CALL: _____

c) ♠ K J 9 8 4
♥ A Q
♦ 3 2
♣ K Q 10 9

VALUATION: _____
CALL: _____

d) ♠ A 9 8 7 6 3
♥ 9 4
♦ Q J 9
♣ 7 2

VALUATION: _____
CALL: _____

e) ♠ K 10 8
♥ 4
♦ A 9
♣ Q J 10 5 4 3 2

VALUATION: ___
CALL: _____

f) ♠ A K
♥ A Q J 10 9
♦ A 8 2
♣ 9 4 3

VALUATION: _____
CALL: _____

g) ♠ A Q 7 3 2
♥ 9 8 7
♦ 5 2
♣ A J 4

VALUATION: _____
CALL: _____

h) ♠ Q J 10 9 2
♥ A Q 7 3 2
♦ 8 2
♣ 4

VALUATION: ___
CALL: _____

i) ♠ 4
♥ K 9 2
♦ A Q 8 7 6 3
♣ Q J 5

VALUATION: _____
CALL: _____

j) ♠ 5 4 2
♥ 10 9 6 5 4 3
♦ A K Q
♣ A

VALUATION: _____
CALL: _____

k) ♠ A Q J
♥ K Q 4
♦ 7 5 4 2
♣ A J 8

VALUATION: ___
CALL: _____

l) ♠ Q J 9 8 6
♥ 3
♦ A K J 5 3
♣ 8 6

VALUATION: _____
CALL: _____

Answers to Quiz – Part II

a) **10 points**. 4 for the ♠A, 3 for the ♥K, 2 for the ♦Q, and 1 for the ♣J.
Pass. The hand has fewer than 13 valuation points.

b) **18 points**. 17 high-card points plus 1 length point for the fifth diamond.
1♦. Open the longest suit.

c) **16 points**. 15 high-card points plus 1 length point for the fifth spade.
1♠. open the longest suit.

d) **9 points**. 7 high-card points plus 2 length points for the six-card spade suit.
Pass. The hand has fewer than 13 valuation points.

e) **13 points**. 10 high-card points plus 3 length points for the seven clubs.
1♣. Open the longest suit.

f) **19 points**. 18 HCPs plus 1 length point for the five-card heart suit.
1♥. Open the longest suit.

g) **12 points**. 11 HCPs plus 1 length point for the fifth spade.
Pass. The hand has fewer than 13 valuation points.

h) **11 points**. 9 HCPs plus 1 length point for the five-card spade suit and 1 length point for the five-card heart suit.
Pass. The hand has fewer than 13 valuation points.

i) **14 points**. 12 high-card points plus 2 length points for the six-card suit.
1♦. Open the longest suit.

j) **15 points**. 13 HCPs plus 2 length points for the six-card heart suit.
1♥. Open the longest suit, not the strongest.

k) **17 points**. All in high cards; no distribution points.
1NT. With no preference for a particular suit, suggest notrump (more on this in the next chapter).

l) **13 points**. 11 high-card points plus 1 length point for the fifth spade and 1 length point for the fifth diamond.
1♠. With a choice between two five-card suits, open the higher-ranking.

Quiz – Part III

How many sure tricks do you have in each of the following suit combinations?

a) DUMMY	b) DUMMY	c) DUMMY	d) DUMMY
♠ A K Q	♥ K 6 5	♦ A Q	♣ Q 9 7 3
DECLARER	DECLARER	DECLARER	DECLARER
♠ 8 5 3	♥ A 3	♦ K J	♣ J 6 4 2

You are on lead with the North hand in the following auction:

WEST	NORTH	EAST	SOUTH
1NT	PASS	PASS	PASS

With each of the following hands, underline the suit you are going to lead and circle the card you'll play against a notrump contract.

e) ♠ K Q J 8 6	f) ♠ 5 3 2	g) ♠ 8 5 4
♥ A 5 3	♥ Q J 10 9	♥ A K 5
♦ 8 7 6	♦ A Q	♦ 8 5
♣ 7 3	♣ Q 8 5 2	♣ K J 6 3 2

You are on lead with the North hand in the following auction:

WEST	NORTH	EAST	SOUTH
1♠	PASS	PASS	PASS

With each of the following hands, underline the suit you are going to lead and circle the card you'll play against a 1♠ contract.

h) ♠ Q 6 4	i) ♠ J 8 2	j) ♠ 9 8 4
♥ A K 9 7	♥ A 7 4	♥ J 8 6 3
♦ J 7 6	♦ K J 7 5 2	♦ Q 9 6 4 3
♣ 7 4 3	♣ Q 4	♣ 8

Answers to Quiz – Part III

a) **Three**. The ♠A, ♠K, and ♠Q.

b) **Two**. The ♥A and ♥K. The high cards don't have to be in the same hand.

c) **Two**. Although you have the four top cards in the suit, they will fall together on two tricks.

d) **Zero**. There are no tricks you can take in this suit without giving up the lead to the opponents.

e) **♠K**. Lead the longest suit against a notrump contract. With a three-card sequence in the suit, lead the highest of the touching cards, the king.

f) **♥Q**. With a choice between suits of equal length, choose the stronger. With a sequence, lead the top of the touching cards, the ♥Q. Partner will know that you don't hold the ♥K but do hold the ♥J and likely the ♥10 as well.

g) **♣3**. The club suit is the longest suit in your hand. With no three-card or longer sequence, lead a low card. Traditionally, the fourth highest card, the ♣3, is led. Partner will know clubs is your longest suit and you do not have a three-card sequence.

h) **♥A**. Against a suit contract you can lead the top of two touching high cards. The lead of the ♥A will tell partner you likely hold the ♥K as well, unless you are leading a short suit.

i) **♦5**. The lead here is not clear cut. With no sequence in any suit, choosing the longest suit is often best. With no touching high cards, start with the fourth highest, the ♦5. If you were to choose to lead a heart, lead the ♥A since you avoid leading a low card against a suit contract holding the ace. If you were to choose to lead a club, lead the ♣Q, top of a two-card suit.

j) **♣8**. Again, the choice of suit is not clear cut. Leading a short suit against a trump contract is a common practice. You are hoping that a second round of the suit will be led before all your trumps are drawn, allowing you to ruff one of declarer's club winners. It would also be reasonable to lead the ♦4 or ♥3 instead.

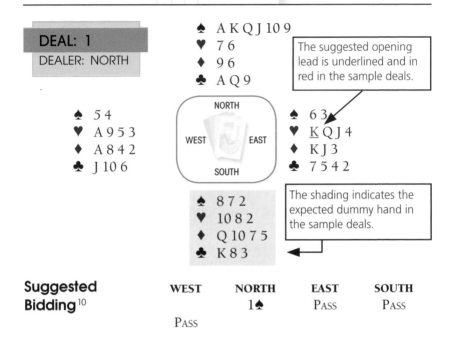

| **DEAL: 1** | |
| DEALER: NORTH | |

♠ A K Q J 10 9
♥ 7 6
♦ 9 6
♣ A Q 9

The suggested opening lead is underlined and in red in the sample deals.

NORTH

WEST   EAST

SOUTH

♠ 5 4
♥ A 9 5 3
♦ A 8 4 2
♣ J 10 6

♠ 6 3
♥ K Q J 4
♦ K J 3
♣ 7 5 4 2

♠ 8 7 2
♥ 10 8 2
♦ Q 10 7 5
♣ K 8 3

The shading indicates the expected dummy hand in the sample deals.

Suggested Bidding [10]	**WEST**	**NORTH**	**EAST**	**SOUTH**
		1♠	PASS	PASS
	PASS			

North is the dealer and values the hand, counting 16 high-card points plus 2 length points for the six-card spade suit. With more than 13 points, North has enough to open the bidding. By bidding 1♠, North suggests spades as the trump suit in exchange for committing the partnership to take at least seven tricks.

East has 10 valuation points, not enough strength to contest the auction by making an overcall. To suggest hearts as the trump suit, for example, East would have to bid at the two level, moving up the Bidding Ladder. Instead, East passes.

South is the responder to North, the opening bidder. South accepts North's choice of a trump suit by passing.

West has only 9 high card points and, like East, doesn't have enough strength or a long enough suit to enter the auction for the partnership. West passes.

The three passes following the opening bid end the auction. The

---

[10] The bidding would be the same in auction or contract bridge.

contract is 1♠. North, the declarer, has contracted to take at least seven tricks with spades as the trump suit.

Suggested Opening Lead

North is declarer. East makes the opening lead. East leads the ♥K, top of the solid sequence.

Declarer's Plan

After East makes the opening lead, South puts the dummy hand face up on the table and North makes a plan.

North's goal is to take at least seven tricks to make the

```
┌──── DECLARER'S PLAN—THE ABC'S ────┐

Declarer: North    Contract: 1♠

ASSESS THE SITUATION          ┌──────────────┐
Goal                    7     │ Declarer has │
Sure Tricks             9     │ more than    │
Extra Tricks Needed     0  ◄──│ enough tricks.│
                              └──────────────┘
BROWSE DECLARER'S CHECKLIST
• Not applicable, no extra tricks
  needed

CONSIDER THE ORDER
• Draw trumps first.
• Take the tricks and run.
```

contract. North counts the sure tricks available from the North and South hands. There are six sure spade tricks and three sure club tricks, for a total of nine tricks. That's more than enough. All declarer has to do is take the tricks and make the contract.

East's ♥K will win the first trick. West doesn't need to play the ♥A since partner's ♥K is good enough. Declarer plays a low heart from the dummy and a low heart from the North hand. West is likely to continue by leading the ♥Q and this will also win a trick since declarer has to follow suit from both hands. When East leads a third round of hearts, however, declarer has no hearts left and trumps in the North hand. Declarer wins the trick.

With enough tricks to make the contract, North starts with the trump suit, playing high spades until the defenders have none left. By drawing the defenders' trumps, declarer makes sure that the defenders can't trump any of the club winners. It won't matter on this deal, but it's a good habit for declarer to follow. Once the defenders' trumps are drawn, it is safe for declarer to take the three sure tricks in the club suit. Together with the six spade winners, declarer has nine tricks.

North-South make the contract of 1♠ with two extra tricks, or overtricks.

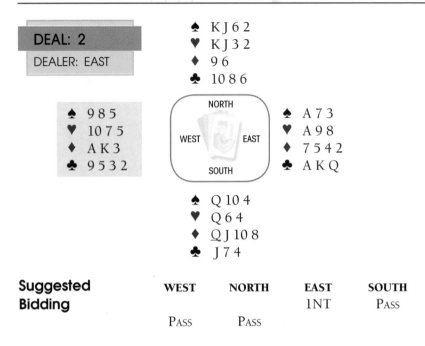

DEAL: 2
DEALER: EAST

♠ K J 6 2
♥ K J 3 2
♦ 9 6
♣ 10 8 6

WEST
♠ 9 8 5
♥ 10 7 5
♦ A K 3
♣ 9 5 3 2

EAST
♠ A 7 3
♥ A 9 8
♦ 7 5 4 2
♣ A K Q

SOUTH
♠ Q 10 4
♥ Q 6 4
♦ Q J 10 8
♣ J 7 4

Suggested Bidding

WEST	NORTH	EAST	SOUTH
		1NT	PASS
PASS	PASS		

East, the dealer, has 17 high-card points. The longest suit is the weak four-card diamond suit, so East suggests playing with no trump suit by opening 1NT.

South has 8 high-card points, not enough to enter the auction for the partnership.

West has 7 high-card points and, satisfied with East's notrump contract, passes.

North has 8 high-card points, not enough to compete for the contract. North passes.

The three successive passes end the auction and the contract is 1NT with East as the declarer. East has to take seven tricks in notrump.

Suggested Opening Lead

South, on declarer's left, is on lead against the 1NT contract. South chooses to lead a diamond, the longest suit. South leads the ♦Q, top of the three-card sequence.

Declarer's Plan

South makes the opening lead and the West hand comes down as the dummy. East makes a plan. East's goal is to take at least seven tricks. There is one sure spade winner, the ♠A, one heart, the ♥A, two diamonds, dummy's ♦A and ♦K, and three club winners, the ♣A, ♣K, and ♣Q. Since

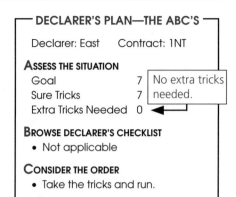

```
┌─ DECLARER'S PLAN—THE ABC'S ─┐
│  Declarer: East    Contract: 1NT │
│  ASSESS THE SITUATION            │
│    Goal             7  ┌──────────┐
│    Sure Tricks      7  │No extra tricks
│    Extra Tricks Needed  0 ◄──┘ needed. │
│  BROWSE DECLARER'S CHECKLIST     │
│    • Not applicable              │
│  CONSIDER THE ORDER              │
│    • Take the tricks and run.    │
└──────────────────────────────────┘
```

seven tricks are available, East has all the tricks that are required to make the contract.

After winning the first trick with dummy's ♦K, declarer can take the sure tricks and make the contract.

Declarer can actually make an extra trick. After winning the first trick with dummy's ♦A or ♦K, declarer could next take the ♣A, ♣K, and ♣Q. All the missing clubs have appeared and dummy's remaining ♣9 is a winner. Declarer then plays another diamond and dummy's high diamond wins. Now declarer can play the ♣9. Since there are no clubs left in the other hands, the ♣9 will win a trick. Declarer finishes with eight tricks.

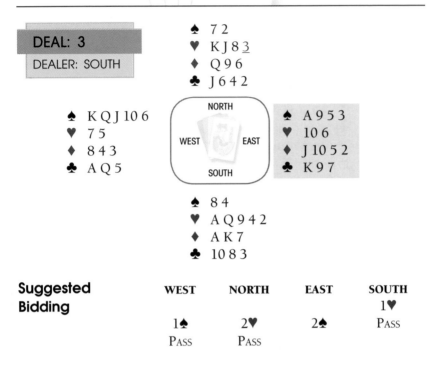

DEAL: 3
DEALER: SOUTH

NORTH
♠ 7 2
♥ K J 8 3
♦ Q 9 6
♣ J 6 4 2

WEST
♠ K Q J 10 6
♥ 7 5
♦ 8 4 3
♣ A Q 5

EAST
♠ A 9 5 3
♥ 10 6
♦ J 10 5 2
♣ K 9 7

SOUTH
♠ 8 4
♥ A Q 9 4 2
♦ A K 7
♣ 10 8 3

Suggested Bidding

WEST	NORTH	EAST	SOUTH
			1♥
1♠	2♥	2♠	PASS
PASS	PASS		

South is the dealer and has 13 high-card points and can add 1 length point for the five-card suit. That's enough to open the bidding. South opens 1♥, the longest suit, suggesting hearts as the trump suit.

The auction moves clockwise to West who has 13 valuation points: 12 high-card points plus 1 length point for the five-card spade suit. With a good five-card suit, West has enough to compete for the contract and overcalls 1♠. West doesn't have to increase the level of the auction since spades are higher-ranking than hearts.

The auction moves to North who is the responder after South opens. North has 7 high-card points. North likes partner's suggestion of hearts as the trump suit. North can compete for the contract by bidding 2♥, moving up the Bidding Ladder to the two level.

Now it is East's turn, the partner of the overcaller. East has 8 high-card points and likes West's choice of spades as the trump suit. East can compete for the contract by bidding 2♠. Because spades are higher-ranking than hearts, East doesn't need to go to the three level.

South doesn't have much more than was shown by opening the

bidding. Unwilling to go to the three level, South passes. West has no reason to bid any more since the partnership is already winning the auction. West passes. North is also unwilling to bid any higher for the privilege of naming the trump suit.

The three successive passes end the auction. The East-West partnership has won the contract. West will be declarer since West first mentioned spades for the partnership.

Suggested Opening Lead

North, on declarer's left, makes the opening lead. Since the partnership has bid hearts during the auction, North would lead a low heart, the ♥3, fourth highest.

Declarer's Plan

North leads and the East hand comes down as the dummy. West, as declarer, makes a plan. West's goal is to take at least eight tricks, the number bid for the privilege of naming trumps.

West counts the combined sure tricks. The partnership has five spade tricks and three club tricks. That's enough to fulfill the obligation. Declarer doesn't need to look further.

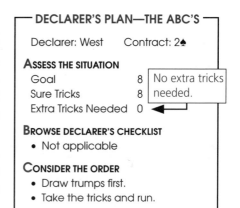

DECLARER'S PLAN—THE ABC'S

Declarer: West   Contract: 2♠

ASSESS THE SITUATION
Goal   8
Sure Tricks   8
Extra Tricks Needed   0

No extra tricks needed.

BROWSE DECLARER'S CHECKLIST
• Not applicable

CONSIDER THE ORDER
• Draw trumps first.
• Take the tricks and run.

After North leads the ♥3 and declarer plays a heart from dummy, South plays the ♥A, third hand high, winning the first trick as West follows suit. South can take the ♦A and ♦K, since the defenders have two tricks in that suit. Then South will probably lead another heart, returning the suit led by partner. The defenders can win a second heart trick but declarer ruffs the third round.

After winning a trick, declarer should draw the defenders' trumps by taking spade winners until the defenders have no spades left. Now it is safe to take the sure club tricks. Declarer has eight tricks, enough to make the contract.

DEAL: 4		♠ A K 7 6 3
DEALER: WEST		♥ J 4
		♦ 8 5 3
		♣ 9 7 3

	NORTH	
♠ Q J 2		♠ 10 9 4
♥ 8 6	WEST EAST	♥ 7 5 2
♦ J 10 9 6		♦ A K 4 2
♣ A Q 8 5	SOUTH	♣ K 10 6

♠ 8 5
♥ A K Q 10 9 3
♦ Q 7
♣ J 4 2

Suggested Bidding	**WEST**	**NORTH**	**EAST**	**SOUTH**
	PASS	PASS	PASS	1♥
	PASS	1♠	PASS	2♥
	PASS	PASS	PASS	

West is the dealer and passes. There are 10 valuation points, all in high cards, not enough to open the bidding.

North passes. North has 8 high-card points plus 1 length point for the five-card suit for a total of 9 valuation points, not enough to open the bidding.

East also has fewer than 13 points and passes. East has 10 valuation points, all in high cards.

South has the last opportunity to open the bidding. South has 12 high-card points plus 2 length points for the six-card suit. The total of 14 valuation points is enough to open. South bids 1♥, suggesting hearts as the trump suit. West passes.

North is the responder to the opening bidder. North doesn't much like South's choice of trump suit and suggests spades as trumps by responding 1♠. East passes.

South much prefers hearts as the trump suit and sends this message by repeating the suit. Over the 1♠ response, South has to bid 2♥ because hearts are lower-ranking than spades. West passes.

Having already suggested spades as trumps, North now settles for hearts as the trump suit by passing. East passes and the auction is over.

South suggested hearts as the strain for the contract and becomes the declarer. North-South have contracted for at least eight tricks.

Suggested Opening Lead

West, to declarer's left, makes the opening lead. With a choice of suits to lead, West might choose the suit that has the solid three-card sequence. West leads the ◆J, top of the sequence.

Declarer's Plan

After West makes the opening lead, the North hand comes down as the dummy. South is the declarer in a contract of 2♥ and has to take eight tricks.

South's first step is to assess the situation and count the sure tricks. The partnership has two spade tricks, the ♠A and ♠K, and six heart tricks, the ♥A, ♥K, ♥Q, ♥J, ♥10, and ♥9. That's all that are required. Declarer doesn't need to look for extra tricks.

> ### DECLARER'S PLAN—THE ABC'S
>
> Declarer: South   Contract: 2♥
>
> **ASSESS THE SITUATION**
> | | |
> |---|---|
> | Goal | 8 |
> | Sure Tricks | 8 |
> | Extra Tricks Needed | 0 |
>
> No extra tricks needed.
>
> **BROWSE DECLARER'S CHECKLIST**
> - Not applicable
>
> **CONSIDER THE ORDER**
> - Draw trumps first.
> - Take the tricks and run.

From the opening lead of the ◆J, East knows that West doesn't hold the ◆Q. Since it isn't in dummy, declarer must hold that card. When a low diamond is played from dummy, East can win the trick with the ◆K and may choose to take a second trick with the ◆A. When South's ◆Q falls on the second round, East might play a third round to make declarer use up a trump.

South can trump the third round of diamonds and start taking the sure tricks. Since there is a trump suit, declarer should begin with hearts, drawing out the defenders' trumps. It will then be perfectly safe to take the spade winners, although it won't actually matter on this deal.

The first game of contract bridge was played aboard the cruise ship Finland that sailed from San Francisco in October 1925. The brainchild of Harold S. Vanderbilt, the new scoring system was tested by Vanderbilt, Francis M. Bacon II, Dudley Pickman Jr. and Frederic Allen and soon became the rage at such fashionable summer resorts as Newport and Southampton.

—AMERICAN CONTRACT BRIDGE LEAGUE BULLETIN,

DECEMBER 1975

Notrump Opening Bids and Responses

The 1NT Opening Bid

The first priority for choosing among possible opening bids at the one level is 1NT. This opening bid is very precise. It is limited to a narrow three-point range and specific distribution. This usually makes it easy for the partnership to find the best contract. An opening 1NT bid requires two features:

OPENING 1 NT

15, 16, or 17 valuation points
A Balanced Hand

The Strength

The precise three-point range is a matter of partnership agreement. Some players use 16–18 points; some use 12–14 points; some use other ranges. 15–17 is a popular range in North America and many other countries, as well as on the Internet. This will be used throughout this series.

Balanced and Unbalanced Hands

A hand is often described by the number of cards held in each suit. There are terms for short suits:

- A *void*: zero cards in a suit.
- A *singleton*: one card in a suit.
- A *doubleton*: two cards in a suit.

The overall distribution of the suits in a hand can be described as *balanced* or *unbalanced*. A balanced hand is one that has no void, no singleton, and at most one doubleton. All other hands are considered unbalanced. There are only three balanced distributions, or *patterns*:

1. A hand with one 4-card suit and three 3-card suits.

♠ K 8 6 3
♥ Q 7 5
♦ A J 7
♣ K Q 3

This balanced hand has no voids, singletons, or doubletons.

2. A hand with two 4-card suits, a 3-card suit, and a doubleton.

♠ A J
♥ A Q 7
♦ K 10 8 4
♣ Q 9 7 3

A hand with only one doubleton is balanced.

3. A hand with one 5-card suit, two 3-card suits, and a doubleton.

♠ K 9 4
♥ J 8 2
♦ A Q 7 5 3
♣ A Q

This balanced hand has a five-card suit, two three-card suits, and one doubleton.

Examples

The following hands meet the requirements for a 1NT opening bid:

♠ Q J 10 8 ♥ 7 6 4 ♦ A K J ♣ A Q 7	There are 17 high-card points. The hand is balanced with one four-card suit and three three-card suits.
♠ 7 3 ♥ A J 4 ♦ K Q 10 2 ♣ A J 7 6	This hand has 15 high-card points. It is balanced with two four-card suits, a three-card suit, and a doubleton. There do not have to be high cards in every suit.
♠ A 8 4 ♥ J 9 7 ♦ Q 8 ♣ A K J 8 4	This hand is worth 16 valuation points. There are 15 high-card points plus 1 length point for the five-card suit. The hand is balanced with one five-card suit, two three-card suits, and a doubleton.

The following hands do not meet the requirements for a 1NT opening bid:

♠ A 7 5 ♥ A 8 2 ♦ K J 7 4 ♣ Q 7 6	The hand is balanced but has only 14 high-card points. It is not strong enough to open 1NT. Instead open 1♦, the longest suit.
♠ A 5 ♥ A J 4 ♦ K Q 10 ♣ A 10 7 4 3	There are 18 high-card points plus 1 length point for the five-card club suit. The hand is balanced but too strong to open 1NT. It would be opened 1♣, the longest suit.

♠ 4
♥ A Q 10 7 5
♦ Q 4 3
♣ A K J 8

The hand is worth 17 valuation points. There are 16 high-card points plus 1 length point for the five-card suit. The hand, however, is unbalanced because it has a singleton. It would be opened 1♥, the longest suit.

Responding to an Opening Bid of 1NT

The partner of the 1NT opening bidder is the responder and is responsible for deciding whether the partnership has enough to go for a bonus level or to be satisfied with a partscore contract.

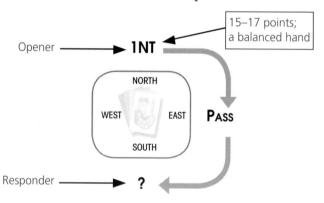

Responder knows more about the combined partnership assets than the 1NT opener. It's the player who knows more who makes the decision, not the player with the stronger hand. On the first bid, opener knows only the cards in opener's hand. Responder knows that opener has a balanced hand with 15–17 points and knows what is in responder's hand. Responder makes two decisions:

- How High the partnership should bid.

- Where the contract should be played.

Deciding How High

Responder first considers How High and decides whether the partnership has enough strength to get to a bonus level. The decision is a matter of addition. About 25–26 combined points are required for a game. Responder knows that opener can contribute 15–17 points.

- If responder has 0–7 points, the partnership belongs in partscore. Even if opener has a maximum of 17 points, the combined partnership value is at most 24 points, not enough for a game bonus.

- If responder has 8 or 9 points, there might be a game. If opener has only 15 points, the partnership has at most 24 points and belongs in partscore. If opener has 16 or 17 points, the partnership probably has enough for a game contract.

- If responder has 10 or more points, the combined total is enough to bid to a game contract. Even if opener has the minimum of 15 points, the partnership has at least 25 combined points.

- If responder has 16 or more points, there might be enough combined strength to go for the slam bonus, but that will be left for POPULAR CONVENTIONS.

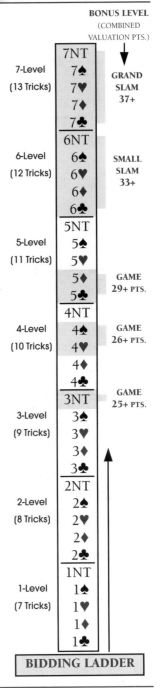

BONUS LEVEL
(COMBINED VALUATION PTS.)

7-Level (13 Tricks)	7NT 7♠ 7♥ 7♦ 7♣	GRAND SLAM 37+
6-Level (12 Tricks)	6NT 6♠ 6♥ 6♦ 6♣	SMALL SLAM 33+
5-Level (11 Tricks)	5NT 5♠ 5♥ 5♦ 5♣	GAME 29+ PTS.
4-Level (10 Tricks)	4NT 4♠ 4♥ 4♦ 4♣	GAME 26+ PTS.
3-Level (9 Tricks)	3NT 3♠ 3♥ 3♦ 3♣	GAME 25+ PTS.
2-Level (8 Tricks)	2NT 2♠ 2♥ 2♦ 2♣	
1-Level (7 Tricks)	1NT 1♠ 1♥ 1♦ 1♣	

BIDDING LADDER

RESPONDER'S POINTS	How High?
0–7 points	Partscore
8–9 points	Maybe game
10 or more points	Game

Deciding Where

The decision on **Where** is also a matter of addition. Responder wants to find a trump fit, typically eight or more combined cards. Since the 1NT opening bid has promised a balanced hand, responder knows that opener has at least two cards in any suit, probably three, possibly four, and occasionally five.

- If responder has a six-card suit, the partnership has at least an eight-card fit.
- If responder has a five-card suit, the partnership probably has an eight-card fit. If opener has three or more cards in the suit, there is a fit. If opener has only a doubleton, there will be an acceptable, if not desirable, seven-card fit.[11]

RESPONDER'S SUIT	EIGHT-CARD FIT?
6 cards or longer	Yes
5 cards	Maybe

Putting How High and Where Together

Even if the partnership does have an eight-card or longer fit, the decision on **Where** to play the contract depends on **How High** the partnership belongs. This is because it takes more tricks to make a game contract in a minor suit, clubs or diamonds, than in a major suit, hearts or spades, or in notrump.

If the partnership belongs in partscore:

---

[11] Finding an eight-card major suit fit when responder has four will be left until Popular Conventions.

- When responder has a five-card suit there is likely to be an eight-card fit; when responder has a six-card or longer suit, there is definitely an eight-card fit. Responder generally chooses to play partscore in the trump suit, rather than 1NT[12].

If the partnership belongs in game:

- When there is an eight-card or longer major suit fit, responder generally chooses to play game in the major suit, rather than 3NT. Although 3NT requires only nine tricks and 4♥ or 4♠ requires ten tricks, the trump fit will usually produce at least one extra trick, and sometimes two or more.
- When there is an eight-card or longer fit in a minor suit, responder ordinarily chooses to play game in 3NT, rather than in the minor suit. A contract of 5♣ or 5♦ requires eleven tricks and the partnership will need at least 28 or 29 combined points. A contract of 3NT requires only nine tricks and can usually be made with as few as 25 or 26 points.

When Responder Knows How HIGH and WHERE

Because the opening 1NT bid is so descriptive, responder will usually know whether the partnership belongs in partscore or at a bonus level and which strain to choose. Here are some examples:

WHEN RESPONDER HAS 10 OR MORE VALUATION POINTS

When responder holds 10 or more points, the partnership has enough combined strength to try for a game bonus since the 1NT opening bid has promised at least 15 points. Responder can then choose the best game contract[13].

---

[12] The 2♣ response is reserved for the *Stayman Convention*, which is beyond the scope of this book. So, even with an eight-card fit in clubs, responder leaves the partnership in a partscore of 1NT.

[13] Slam bidding is discussed in the third book of this series, POPULAR CONVENTIONS.

Your partner opens 1NT ◄——— 15–17 points; a balanced hand

You are the responder with the following hands:

♠ K J 3
♥ A J 8 7 4 3
♦ 3
♣ 8 5 2

How High? *Game.* You have 11 valuation points: 9 high-card points plus 2 length points for the six-card suit. The partnership has at least 26 combined points (15 + 11).

Where? Hearts. You have six hearts and opener has at least two so there is an eight-card or longer fit. With a choice between game in a major suit and notrump responder chooses the major suit.

Decision: 4♥. Put the partnership in a game contract with hearts as the trump suit. You will be declarer and have to take ten tricks.

♠ A 4 3
♥ J 5 3
♦ Q 7 5
♣ K 9 4 2

How High? Game. You have 10 high-card points so the partnership has at least 25.

Where? Notrump. The partnership is unlikely to have an eight-card fit in a major suit.

Decision: 3NT. Put the partnership in a game contract with no trump suit. Opener will be declarer and have to take nine tricks.

♠ Q 10 5
♥ 9
♦ K Q 9 7 5
♣ Q J 9 7

How High? Game. You have 10 high-card points plus 1 length point for the fifth diamond. There are at least 26 combined points so go for the game bonus.

Where? Notrump. The partnership is unlikely to have an eight-card fit in spades. There is probably an eight-card or longer fit in diamonds or clubs but, with a choice between 5♣ or 5♦ and 3NT, responder generally chooses the nine-trick game, 3NT. Although opener needs a balanced hand to bid 1NT, responder doesn't need a balanced hand to put the partnership in game in notrump.

Decision: 3NT. Partner will be declarer and have to take nine tricks to make the contract.

WHEN RESPONDER HAS 0–7 VALUATION POINTS

When responder holds 7 or fewer points, the partnership doesn't have enough combined strength to try for a game bonus. For example:

| **Your partner opens 1 NT** ◄——— 15–17 points; a balanced hand |

♠ K 7
♥ Q 8 6
♦ 8 5 4 3
♣ J 9 6 2

How High? Partscore. You have 6 high-card points so the partnership has at most 23 points (17 + 6) and could have as few as 21 (15 + 6).

Where? Notrump. It's possible the partnership has an eight-card fit, but responder typically doesn't assume there is a fit unless holding a five-card or longer suit.

Decision: Pass. Leave the partnership in a partscore contract of 1NT. Partner, opener, will have to take seven tricks to make the contract.

♠ 6 4
♥ Q 8 7 5 4 3
♦ 8 5
♣ J 10 4

How High? Partscore. You have 3 high-card points plus 2 length points for the six-card suit. The partnership has at most 22 points.

Where? Hearts. Opener has at least two hearts so the partnership has an eight-card fit.

Decision: 2♥. Put the partnership in a partscore contract with hearts as trumps. You will be declarer and have to take eight tricks.

♠ 3
♥ 9 6 4
♦ 8 6 5 4 3 2
♣ 10 8 7

How High? Partscore. You have 2 length points for the six-card diamond suit. The partnership has at most 19 combined points.

Where? Diamonds. There is an eight-card or longer fit because opener has at least two diamonds. With a choice in partscore between a suit and 1NT, responder chooses the suit.

Decision: 2♦. Responder doesn't need any high-card points to put the partnership in the best partscore contract. You'll be declarer. Even if you can't take eight tricks with diamonds as trumps, it will likely be better than leaving partner to take seven tricks in 1NT.

When Responder Doesn't Know How High

With 8 or 9 points, responder needs more information to decide whether the partnership belongs in partscore or game. For example:

WHEN RESPONDER HAS 8–9 VALUATION POINTS

| Your partner opens 1 NT | ◄— | 15–17 points; a balanced hand |

♠ K 7 3
♥ J 10 2
♦ K Q 9 5
♣ 10 8 7

How High? Maybe game. You have 9 high-card points. If opener has 15 valuation points, the partnership will have only 24 combined points, not quite enough to go for the game bonus. If opener has 17 points, the partnership has 26 combined points, enough to try for a game contract.

Where? Notrump. There is unlikely to be an eight-card major suit fit. Even if there is an eight-card or longer minor suit fit, the partnership won't have enough combined strength to go for the eleven-trick game contract in a minor suit. Better to play in a notrump contract.

Decision: 2NT. Responder moves toward game without actually bidding it. This bid invites opener to continue to game with the top of the range for the 1NT opening. With the bottom of the range, opener can pass and stop in partscore.

When Responder Doesn't Know Where [14]

WITH A FIVE-CARD MAJOR SUIT

There are times when responder needs more information to decide whether the partnership has an eight-card or longer trump fit. For example:

| Your partner opens 1NT | ◄— | 15–17 points; a balanced hand |

---

[14] The Stayman Convention (2♣ response) is an artificial bid that helps responder get more information from opener before deciding how high and where the contract should be played. It's beyond the scope of this book (see POPULAR CONVENTIONS in this series).

♠ 6 2
♥ K J 10 8 2
♦ 7 5 4
♣ A Q 2

How High? Game. You have 11 points: 10 high-card points plus 1 length point for the five-card suit. The partnership has at least 26 combined points.

Where? Maybe hearts. There will be an eight-card fit if opener has three or more hearts. That would make 4♥ the best game contract. If opener has only two hearts, however, there's only a seven-card fit and 3NT would likely be the best contract.

Decision: 3♥. This response asks opener to bid again and choose between game in notrump and game in hearts. With three or more hearts, opener can bid 4♥, going for the ten-trick contract with hearts as the trump suit. With only two hearts, opener bids 3NT, settling for the nine-trick game contract.

Opener's Rebid After Opening 1NT

Opener's second bid is called the *rebid*. On most hands, responder can immediately make the decision about **How High** and **Where** to play the contract.

- On the rebid, opener passes.

Occasionally, responder asks for further information about opener's exact strength or distribution. For now, there are only two situations when opener has to make a decision about the rebid:

- The first is when responder bids 2NT, asking opener to help decide **How High**. Opener can pass with a minimum hand (15), bid 3NT with a maximum hand (17), and choose whether to bid or pass with an in-between hand (16).
- The second situation is when responder bids 3♥ or 3♠, asking opener to help make the decision about **Where** the contract should be played. With only two cards in the five-card major suit suggested by responder, opener's decision is to play in 3NT. With three or more cards in responder's major suit, opener bids a game in the major.

The Bidding Messages

How does opener know whether to pass responder's bid or whether to bid again?

The Bidding Messages

Each bid made during the bidding conversation carries one of three possible messages:

- **Signoff**. A signoff bid asks partner to pass.
- **Invitational**. An invitational bid invites partner to continue on to game with the top of the range shown by previous bids but to pass with the bottom of the range.
- **Forcing**. A forcing bid asks partner to bid again and to further describe the hand.

The Bidding Messages After a 1NT Opening Bid

- **Signoff**. The responses of 2♦, 2♥, and 2♠ to opener's 1NT bid are all signoff bids; responder has decided to play in partscore. The key point is that after a 1NT opening bid, responder with very few points can suggest a better contract at the two level. Playing in the partnership's long suit is better than playing in notrump.

  Similarly, responder's bids of 3NT, 4♥, and 4♠ are all signoff bids; responder has decided to play in a game contract and has chosen the appropriate game contract.

- **Invitational**. The response of 2NT to opener's 1NT bid is an invitational bid. Responder is inviting opener to bid 3NT with the top of the range, 17 points, but pass with the bottom of the range, 15 points. With 16 points, opener can decide whether to accept or reject the invitation.

- **Forcing**. The responses of 3♥ or 3♠ to opener's 1NT bid are forcing bids. Responder is asking opener to choose between game in notrump and game in the major suit. Responder isn't expecting opener to pass.

Both opener's and responder's bids carry a message. For example, the opening bid of 1NT is invitational. Responder can pass with 7 or fewer points and a hand suitable for play in a partscore of 1NT. Or, responder can choose another contract. Opener's 1NT is not a signoff or a forcing bid; it is invitational.

Becoming familiar with the bidding message assigned to each bid is the key to conducting a smooth bidding conversation to a reasonable contract with no surprises for either partner.

Declarer's Plan – The ABC's

Assess the Situation

- Goal
- Sure Tricks
- Extra Tricks Needed

When there are already enough sure tricks to reach the goal, declarer goes ahead and takes them. If there are not enough sure tricks, declarer moves to the second step of the plan.

Browse Declarer's Checklist to Develop Extra Tricks

There are three ways for declarer (or the defenders) to develop extra tricks in both notrump and trump contracts.

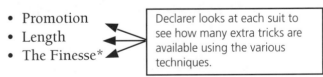

- Promotion
- Length
- The Finesse*

Declarer looks at each suit to see how many extra tricks are available using the various techniques.

*The finesse is discussed in Chapter 4.

Let's look at the first two techniques.

PROMOTION

One way to develop extra tricks is through *promotion*, turning cards into winners by driving out all the higher-ranking cards. To use promotion, look touching cards. They can be easy to spot when the high cards are in the same hand. For example:

DUMMY
♥ 3 2

DECLARER
♥ K Q

There are no sure tricks in this suit, since the opponents hold the ♥A. Declarer, however, can lead one of the high cards to drive out the defenders' ♥A. This promotes the remaining high card into a winner.

DUMMY
♦ Q 6 2

DECLARER
♦ K J 5

When the high cards are not in the same hand, it's more of a challenge to see the opportunity for promotion. The high cards don't have to be in the same hand. Declarer can promote two winners in this suit by leading dummy's ♦Q or by leading the ♦K or ♦J from declarer's hand.

DUMMY
♣ Q 9 7 4

DECLARER
♣ J 10 5 2

In this example declarer is missing both the ♣A and ♣K but can promote two winners. Use one of the high cards to drive out one of the defenders' high cards. After regaining the lead, use another high card to drive out the defenders' other high card. Declarer's remaining high cards have now been promoted into winners. The lead has to be given up twice, but if declarer needs extra tricks, this is one way to get them.

Now let's look at a second technique for developing extra tricks.

LENGTH

Declarer may be able to develop tricks through length. If declarer continues to lead a suit until the defenders have no cards left, any remaining cards are winners. To recognize the potential for establishing tricks through length, look for long suits or suits where you have lots of cards in the combined hands. For example:

DUMMY
♦ 8 6 5 2

DECLARER
♦ A K 7 3

In this suit, declarer has two sure tricks, the ♦A and ♦K. If the five missing diamonds are divided 3-2, three cards in one defender's hand and two in the other, declarer can develop a third trick through length.

Declarer wins two tricks with the ♦A and ♦K and plays a third round of the suit, hoping the complete layout is something like this:

DUMMY
♦ 8 6 5 2

DEFENDER   DEFENDER
♦ J 9   ♦ Q 10 4

DECLARER
♦ A K 7 3

The defenders win the third round of the suit with the ♦Q, but when declarer regains the lead and plays the fourth round of diamonds, declarer wins the trick because the defenders have no diamonds left.

The number of tricks that can be developed through length depends on how the missing cards are divided between the defenders' hands. When using this technique, it is useful to have an idea how the outstanding cards are likely to be divided. As a general guideline:

An odd number of missing cards tends to divide as evenly as possible; an even number of missing cards tends to divide slightly unevenly.

NUMBER OF OUTSTANDING CARDS	MOST LIKELY DIVISION
3	2-1
4	3-1
5	3-2
6	4-2
7	4-3
8	5-3

DUMMY
♥ 9 6 4 3

DECLARER
♥ 10 8 7 5 2

There are nine combined cards in hearts in this layout, leaving the defenders with only four. Even if one defender holds the ♥A-K-Q-J, declarer can develop a trick. After leading the suit four times, the defenders will have no hearts left and declarer's remaining heart will be a winner.

It would be unlucky to find one defender with all four of the missing hearts.

DUMMY
♥ 9 6 4 3

DEFENDER   DEFENDER
♥ A Q J   ♥ K

DECLARER
♥ 10 8 7 5 2

If the missing hearts are divided 3-1, as expected, declarer can develop two winners in this suit after the opponents have taken their three tricks. Here is a likely layout of the heart suit.

DUMMY
♥ 9 6 4 3

DEFENDER   DEFENDER
♥ A Q   ♥ K J

DECLARER
♥ 10 8 7 5 2

Declarer will do even better if the missing hearts are divided exactly 2-2. By playing the suit twice, all the defenders' hearts will be removed. Declarer will be left with three winners!

Consider the Order

When it comes to the third stage of the plan, considering the order in which to play the cards, here are two additional guidelines:

1) Develop the extra tricks early. When promoting tricks or developing them through length, you may have to give up the lead to the opponents. It's a good idea to keep sure tricks in the other suits to help regain the lead so that the established winners can be taken. Don't be afraid to lose tricks early.

2) Play the high card from the short side first. When taking sure tricks or promoting winners, look for suits that are unevenly divided between the two hands. They take special care. You may find yourself in the wrong hand at the wrong time. Start by playing the high cards from the hand with the fewer cards.

DUMMY
♠ A Q 5

DECLARER
short side ♠ **K** 4
high card ↗

In this suit, if you win the first trick with dummy's ♠A and win the second trick with the ♠K, you'll be in the wrong hand to take a trick with the ♠Q. Instead, start by winning a trick with the ♠K, the high card from the short side. Then play the ♠4 over to one of dummy's winners and you'll be in the right hand.

DUMMY
short side ♥ **Q** 5
high card ↗

DECLARER
♥ K J 10 2

When promoting winners in a suit like this, start by playing the ♥Q on the first trick, the high card from the short side. If the defenders take the ♥A, the ♥K-J-10 are promoted into three winners. The defenders don't have to take their ♥A on the first round of the suit. If they don't play the ♥A, allowing dummy's ♥Q to win the first trick, declarer can continue by leading the ♥5 and playing a high heart from declarer's hand. If the defenders still refuse to take the ♥A, declarer is in the right hand to lead a third round of the suit to promote one more winner.

Defense – Attitude Signals

A defender can't see partner's hand, only the dummy. That makes it challenging to formulate a plan to defeat the contract. The defenders, however, can try to communicate information about their hands through the cards they choose to play.

You can encourage partner to lead a suit or continue leading a suit by playing the highest card you can afford. You can discourage partner from leading a suit by playing the lowest card.

A high card is an encouraging signal.
A low card is a discouraging signal.

This is called an *attitude signal*. For example, suppose partner leads the ♠Q against a notrump contract and you hold one of these hands:

1)	♠ K 8 2	2)	♠ 8 6 2
	♥ 9 6 3 2		♥ 8 6
	♦ 8 5 4 2		♦ K Q 9 5 2
	♣ 10 4		♣ J 6 3

With the first hand, you like spades and can make an encouraging signal by playing the ♠8, the highest card you can afford. With the second hand, you don't like spades and can show this by making a discouraging signal, the ♠2. In this context, a "high" card is ideally a 7, 8, or 9; a "low" card is a 2, 3, or 4.

You are not, however, always dealt the perfect cards. On the first hand, you might have ♠K-3-2. Now the ♠3 is the highest card you can afford to tell partner you like spades. On the second hand, you might have ♠9-8-7. The ♠7 is the lowest card you have to make a discouraging signal. So, "high" and "low" are relative terms and you have to do the best that you can to tell partner whether or not you like a particular suit.

SUMMARY

Opening 1NT

- 15, 16, or 17 valuation points.
- A balanced hand

Responding to an Opening 1NT Bid

When opener bids 1NT, responder can use the following guidelines to decide How High and Where the partnership belongs[15]:

- With 0–7 points: Bid 2♦, 2♥, or 2♠ with a five-card or longer suit. Otherwise, pass. These are signoff bids.

- With 8–9 points: Bid 2NT with no eight-card or longer major suit fit. This is an invitational bid.

- With 10–15 points: Bid 4♥ or 4♠ with a six-card or longer major suit. These are signoff bids. Bid 3♥ or 3♠ with a five-card major suit. These are forcing bids. Otherwise, bid 3NT. This is a signoff bid. (Slam will be discussed in a later book.)

[15] The forcing 2♣ Stayman convention is discussed in POPULAR CONVENTIONS.

		BONUS LEVEL (COMBINED VALUATION PTS.)
7-Level (13 Tricks)	7NT 7♠ 7♥ 7♦ 7♣	GRAND SLAM 37+
6-Level (12 Tricks)	6NT 6♠ 6♥ 6♦ 6♣	SMALL SLAM 33+
5-Level (11 Tricks)	5NT 5♠ 5♥ 5♦ 5♣	GAME 29+ PTS.
4-Level (10 Tricks)	4NT 4♠ 4♥ 4♦ 4♣	GAME 26+ PTS.
3-Level (9 Tricks)	3NT 3♠ 3♥ 3♦ 3♣	GAME 25+ PTS.
2-Level (8 Tricks)	2NT 2♠ 2♥ 2♦ 2♣	
1-Level (7 Tricks)	1NT 1♠ 1♥ 1♦ 1♣	

BIDDING LADDER

55

Opener's Rebid After a 1NT Opening

- Opener passes when:
  - Responder makes a signoff bid at the two level (2♦, 2♥, 2♠);
  - Responder makes a signoff bid in game (3NT, 4♥, 4♠).
- Opener is invited to bid again if responder bids 2NT. Opener passes with a minimum and bids 3NT with a maximum.
- Opener must bid again if responder bids 3♥ or 3♠. Opener bids game in the major suit with three or more cards in the suit. Otherwise, opener bids 3NT.

Bidding Messages

Signoff	Asks partner to pass.
Invitational:	Invites partner to bid.
Forcing:	Asks partner to bid again.

Declarer's Plan—The ABCs

Assess the Situation
- Goal
- Sure Tricks
- Extra Tricks Needed

Browse Declarer's Checklist if Extra Tricks are Required
- Promotion
- Length
- The Finesse

Consider the Order
- Develop the extra tricks needed to make the contract early.
- Play the high card from the short side first.

Defense—Attitude Signals

You can encourage partner to lead a suit or continue leading a suit by giving an attitude signal when you have a choice of cards to play:
- A high card is an encouraging signal.
- A low card is a discouraging signal.

Quiz – Part I

You are the dealer. What's your call?

a) ♠ A J 10
   ♥ K Q 4
   ♦ Q 10 7 6
   ♣ A 9 4

b) ♠ K 9 4
   ♥ J
   ♦ K Q J 8 4
   ♣ A Q 7 5

c) ♠ K J 7
   ♥ A Q 4
   ♦ Q 2
   ♣ K 10 9 7 3

Partner opens 1NT. **How High** (part score, maybe game, game) and **Where** (suit or notrump) does the partnership belong on each of the following hands? What do you respond?

d) ♠ Q 6 3
   ♥ K 7 3
   ♦ 8 7 4 3
   ♣ 10 4 3

   How High:_____
   Where: _____
   Response: _____

e) ♠ 6 4
   ♥ Q 10 8 7 6 2
   ♦ 10 5 2
   ♣ 8 2

   How High: ____
   Where: _____
   Response: _____

f) ♠ K Q 5
   ♥ K 5 2
   ♦ J 7 5
   ♣ K 9 8 6

   How High: _____
   Where:_____
   Response: _____

g) ♠ A J 9 7 6 4
   ♥ 2
   ♦ K J 4
   ♣ 9 6 5

   How High:_____
   Where: _____
   Response: _____

h) ♠ A 4
   ♥ K J 8
   ♦ J 7 5 4
   ♣ 10 6 5 2

   How High: ____
   Where: _____
   Response: _____

i) ♠ 7 5
   ♥ Q 8 4
   ♦ K 6
   ♣ A J 8 6 4 2

   How High: _____
   Where:_____
   Response: _____

Answers to Quiz – Part I

a) **1NT**. The hand is balanced and has 16 high-card points.

b) **1♦**. The hand has 17 valuation points: 16 high-card points plus 1 length point for the fifth diamond. However, it is unbalanced because it contains a singleton. Open the long suit.

c) **1NT**. The hand is balanced with no singletons or voids and only one doubleton. There are 15 high-card points plus 1 length point.

d) **Partscore**. You have 5 high-card points so the partnership has at most 22 combined points.
   Notrump. There is no five-card or longer suit to suggest as trumps.
   Pass. Leave the partnership in partscore in a notrump contract.

e) **Partscore**. You have 2 high-card points plus 2 length points. There are not enough combined points for game. **Hearts**. Partner has at least two hearts so there is an eight-card fit.
   2♥. Put the partnership in partscore with hearts as trumps.

f) **Game**. You have 12 high-card points so the partnership has at least 27 (15 + 12) points, enough for game.
   Notrump. There is unlikely to be an eight-card major suit fit. **3NT**. Take the partnership to the game bonus level in notrump.

g) **Game**. You have 9 high-card points plus 2 length points.
   Spades. Opener has at least two spades so the partnership has an eight-card fit.
   4♠. Take the partnership to the game bonus level in spades.

h) **Maybe Game**. You have 9 points so the partnership has between 24 (15 + 9) and 26 (17 + 9).
   Notrump. There is unlikely to be an eight-card fit in a major suit.
   2NT. Move toward game. Opener can pass with a minimum.

i) **Game**. You have 10 high-card points plus 2 length points for the six-card suit.
   Notrump. Although you have an eight-card or longer fit in clubs, prefer the nine-trick game contract of 3NT to the eleven-trick contract in a minor suit.
   3NT. Go to the game level in notrump.

Quiz – Part II

Partner opens 1NT. **How High** (partscore, maybe game, game) and **Where** (suit, notrump, not sure) does the partnership belong on each of the following hands? What do you respond?

a) ♠ —	b) ♠ 8 5 3 2	c) ♠ 5 4
♥ 6 4 2	♥ J 7 6 4	♥ K Q 10 4 2
♦ Q J 8 6 4	♦ 8 2	♦ A J 2
♣ J 9 7 4 2	♣ Q 7 4	♣ 10 4 3
How High:_____	How High: ____	How High: _____
Where: _____	Where: _____	Where:_____
Response: _____	Response: _____	Response: _____

What is the bidding message (signoff, invitational, forcing) sent by each of the following responses to 1NT:

   d) 2♥   e) 2NT   f) 3NT   g) 4♥   h) 3♠

You open 1NT with this hand:

              ♠ A J 4
              ♥ 9 6
              ♦ A Q 7 5
              ♣ K J 6 5

What do you rebid if responder bids:

   i) 2♥   j) 2NT   k) 3♥   l) 3NT   m) 4♠

Answers to Quiz – Part II

a) **Partscore**. You have 4 HCPs and 1 length point for each of the five-card suits. Not enough combined strength for game.

Diamonds. You have a five-card diamond suit so the partnership likely has an eight-card fit. You can't suggest clubs because the 2♣ response is reserved.

2♦. Put the partnership in partscore in the likely eight-card fit.

b) **Partscore**. You have 3 high-card points so the partnership has at most 20 (17 + 3).

Notrump. You don't have a five-card or longer suit to suggest as trumps.

Pass. Leave the partnership in 1NT.

c) **Game**. You have 10 high-card points plus 1 length point for the five-card suit.

Maybe hearts. If partner has 3 or more hearts, there is an eight-card fit.

3♥. This response asks opener to choose between 3NT and 4♥.

d) **Signoff**. Opener is expected to pass. Responder has chosen a partscore contract in hearts.

e) **Invitational**. Opener can continue to 3NT with the top of the 1NT range or pass with the bottom of the range.

f) **Signoff**. Opener is expected to pass. Responder has chosen a game contract in notrump.

g) **Signoff**. Opener is expected to pass responder's choice of 4♥.

h) **Forcing**. Opener is being asked to choose between 3NT and 4♠.

i) **Pass**. 2♥ is a signoff bid. Responder wants to play partscore with hearts as the trump suit.

j) **Pass**. 2NT is an invitational bid. With only 15 high-card points you are at the bottom of the range for a 1NT opening.

k) **3NT**. Responder's bid is forcing, asking you to choose between 3NT and 4♥. With a doubleton heart, choose 3NT.

l) **Pass**. Responder has made a signoff bid by choosing to play game in notrump.

m) **Pass**. Responder wants to play in a game contract with spades as trumps.

Quiz – Part III

How many tricks can you promote in each of the following suit combinations?

a) DUMMY
♠ 7 4 3

b) DUMMY
♥ 7 6 4 2

c) DUMMY
♦ Q 5

d) DUMMY
♣ J 10 9 8

DECLARER
♠ K Q J

DECLARER
♥ Q J 10 9

DECLARER
♦ K 3

DECLARER
♣ 7 6 3 2

How would you expect the missing cards to be divided in each of the following suit combinations? How many tricks can you develop through length if the missing cards are divided as expected?

e) DUMMY
♠ 9 7 3 2

f) DUMMY
♥ 10 7 5 4

g) DUMMY
♦ 9 5

h) DUMMY
♣ 6 4 2

DECLARER
♠ 8 6 5 4

DECLARER
♥ 9 8 6 3 2

DECLARER
♦ 8 7 6 4 3 2

DECLARER
♣ 8 7 5 3

DIVISION: _____
TRICKS: _____

DIVISION: _____
TRICKS: _____

DIVISION: _____
TRICKS: _____

DIVISION: _____
TRICKS: _____

You are on defense against a notrump contract and partner leads the ♦Q.

  i) What do you know about partner's diamond suit?
  j) If you hold ♦K-9-2, do you like partner's choice of lead? How can you tell partner?
  k) If you hold ♦7-4-2, do you like partner's choice of lead? How can you tell partner?

Answers to Quiz – Part III

a) **Two**. Lead one of the high spades to drive out the defenders' ♠A, promoting the two remaining high cards as winners.

b) **Two**. After the defenders' ♥A and ♥K have both been driven out, declarer's two remaining hearts will be promoted into winners. Two tricks must be lost.

c) **One**. The high cards don't have to be in the same hand to promote a winner.

d) **One**. Three tricks must be lost to the defenders' ♣A, ♣K, and ♣Q. Declarer's remaining club will then have been promoted into a winner.

e) **3-2**. You expect the five missing cards to divide as evenly as possible.

   One. By leading the suit three times, the remaining spade will be a winner.

f) **3-1**. You expect the four missing hearts to be divided slightly unevenly.

   Two. After the suit is led three times, the defenders should have no hearts left.

g) **3-2**. The five missing cards are likely to divide as evenly as possible.

   Three. Once three tricks have been lost, declarer's remaining three diamonds should be winners.

h) **4-2**. The six missing clubs are most likely to divide slightly unevenly.

   Zero. If a defender has four clubs, no tricks can be developed through length.

i) Partner doesn't hold the ♦K but holds the ♦J and likely the ♦10 as well. Partner probably has at least four cards in the suit.

j) **You like diamonds**. You can play the ♦9 as an encouraging signal.

k) **You don't like diamonds**. You can play the ♦2 as a discouraging signal.

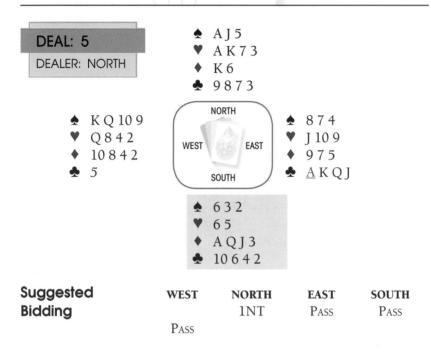

	DEAL: 5	♠ A J 5
	DEALER: NORTH	♥ A K 7 3
		♦ K 6
		♣ 9 8 7 3

♠ K Q 10 9
♥ Q 8 4 2
♦ 10 8 4 2
♣ 5

NORTH
WEST EAST
SOUTH

♠ 8 7 4
♥ J 10 9
♦ 9 7 5
♣ A K Q J

♠ 6 3 2
♥ 6 5
♦ A Q J 3
♣ 10 6 4 2

Suggested
Bidding

WEST	NORTH	EAST	SOUTH
	1NT	Pass	Pass
Pass			

North has 15 high-card points and a balanced hand. There are no voids, no singletons, and only one doubleton. The hand meets the requirements for an opening bid of 1NT.

East has 11 valuation points, all high-card points, not enough strength to contest the auction. East has a good club suit but would have to bid at the two level and contract for eight tricks. East passes.

South, the responder to North's 1NT opening bid, decides **How High** and **Where**. South has 7 high-card points and knows that North has a maximum of 17 valuation points. The partnership has at most 24 combined points. So the answer to **How High** is partscore. South must also decide **Where**. With no five-card or longer suit, South is happy to settle for a notrump contract and not take the partnership beyond the one level. South passes.

West has only 7 high card points, not enough to enter the auction. West passes.

The three successive passes end the auction. The contract is 1NT and the declarer is North. North has contracted to take seven tricks with no trump suit. East-West will try to defeat the contract.

Suggested Opening Lead

Since North is declarer, East makes the opening lead. With a solid sequence in clubs, East leads the ♣A, top of the solid sequence.

Declarer's Plan

After East makes the opening lead, South puts the dummy hand face up on the table.

North's goal is to take at least seven tricks to make the contract. North counts the sure tricks available from the North and South hands. North counts one sure spade trick, two sure heart tricks, and four sure diamond tricks, for a total of seven tricks. That's enough. All

┌─── **DECLARER'S PLAN—THE ABC'S** ───┐

Declarer: North   Contract: 1NT

ASSESS THE SITUATION
Goal	7
Sure Tricks	7
Extra Tricks Needed	0

BROWSE DECLARER'S CHECKLIST
• Not applicable

CONSIDER THE ORDER
• Take the tricks and run.
• High card from the short side first in diamonds.

declarer has to do is take the tricks and make the contract.

East will take the first four club tricks. After that, East has to switch to another suit and may choose the ♥J, top of the sequence, but declarer can win this trick with the ♥K.

Declarer must be careful when taking the diamond winners. If North starts by playing the ♦6 to dummy's ♦A, the second trick in the suit will be won by North's ♦K. Declarer is now in the wrong hand to take the other two diamond winners. The ♦Q and ♦J are stranded. There is no way to get to the dummy hand to take them.

Declarer should start the diamond suit by playing the ♦K, high card from the short side first. After winning this trick, declarer can lead the ♦6 to one of dummy's high diamonds and will be in the right hand at the right time to take the other two diamond winners. Declarer finishes with seven tricks, making the contract.

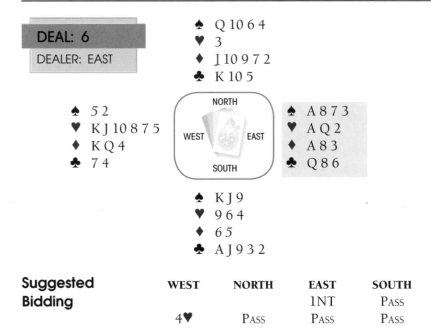

DEAL: 6		♠ Q 10 6 4		
DEALER: EAST		♥ 3		
		♦ J 10 9 7 2		
		♣ K 10 5		

♠ 5 2
♥ K J 10 8 7 5
♦ K Q 4
♣ 7 4

♠ A 8 7 3
♥ A Q 2
♦ A 8 3
♣ Q 8 6

♠ K J 9
♥ 9 6 4
♦ 6 5
♣ A J 9 3 2

Suggested Bidding

WEST	NORTH	EAST	SOUTH
		1NT	Pass
4♥	Pass	Pass	Pass

East is the dealer with 16 high-card points and a balanced hand with no voids, no singletons, and no doubletons. The hand falls into the range for an opening bid of 1NT.

South has 9 high-card points plus 1 length point for the five-card suit, not enough to enter the auction at the two level. South passes.

West has 9 high-card points plus 2 length points for the six-card heart suit, a total of 11 valuation points. West decides **How High**. East's 1NT opening bid has promised at least 15 points, so West knows the partnership has at least 26 combined points. That's enough to go for the game bonus.

West decides **Where**. West has six hearts and East must hold at least two hearts, otherwise East would not have a balanced hand. West knows the partnership has at least an eight-card fit in hearts. Knowing the partnership has a suitable trump suit and enough strength for a game bonus, West bids 4♥.

North passes. East respects partner's choice of contract and passes. South passes and the auction is over.

East-West have contracted for 10 tricks with hearts as the trump suit. Since West first mentioned hearts, West will be the declarer.

Suggested Opening Lead

North, on declarer's left, is on lead against the 4♥ contract. North leads the ♦J, top of the solid sequence in that suit.

Declarer's Plan

After North makes the opening lead and the East hand comes down as the dummy, West makes a plan. As declarer, West's goal is to take at least ten tricks to make the 4♥ contract. West begins by counting the sure winners: one spade, six sure heart winners, and three diamonds. That's a total of ten, exactly what is required.

> ┌─ DECLARER'S PLAN—THE ABC'S ─┐
>
> Declarer: West   Contract: 4♥
>
> **A**SSESS THE SITUATION
> Goal   10
> Sure Tricks   10
> Extra Tricks Needed   0
>
> **B**ROWSE DECLARER'S CHECKLIST
> Not applicable
>
> **C**ONSIDER THE ORDER
> • Draw trumps first.
> • Take the tricks and run.

With enough tricks to make the contract, declarer's first priority is to draw trumps. After winning the first diamond trick, declarer starts taking heart winners. Declarer continues taking heart winners until the defenders have no trumps remaining. This will take three rounds because South holds three trumps.

Once the defenders' trumps are drawn, it is safe to take the winners in the other suits. West will finish with 10 tricks and East-West will receive the game bonus for bidding and making a contract of 4♥.

If declarer tried to take the diamond winners before drawing all the defenders' trumps, South would ruff the third diamond trick with a low heart. Now declarer would have only nine tricks and would be defeated in the 4♥ contract.

DEAL: 7

DEALER: SOUTH

```
            ♠ A 5 2
            ♥ 8 4 3 2
            ♦ Q 10
            ♣ K J 6 2
```

```
                    NORTH
♠ 6 3                                   ♠ Q J 10 9 8 7
♥ A K 7                                 ♥ 9 5
♦ A K 6 3 2     WEST        EAST        ♦ 7 4
♣ Q 9 4                                 ♣ 8 5 3
                    SOUTH
```

```
            ♠ K 4
            ♥ Q J 10 6
            ♦ J 9 8 5
            ♣ A 10 7
```

Suggested Bidding

WEST	NORTH	EAST	SOUTH
			PASS
1NT	PASS	2♠	PASS
PASS	PASS		

South is the dealer and has 11 points in high cards, not enough to open.

The auction moves to West who has 17 valuation points: 16 high-card points plus 1 length point for the five-card diamond suit. West has a balanced hand with no voids or singletons and only one doubleton. These are the requirements for an opening bid of 1NT.

North has 10 high-card points, not enough to enter the auction. The bidding moves to East.

East has 3 high-card points plus 2 length points for the six-card suit. East decides **HOW HIGH**. Since West holds at most 17 points for the 1NT opening bid, East knows the partnership has at most 22 combined valuation points, not enough to go for a game bonus. The partnership should stop in partscore. East still has to decide **WHERE**.

West's 1NT opening bid shows a balanced hand, so West must hold at least a doubleton spade. Since East has a six-card suit, the partnership has at least an eight-card fit in spades. The partnership belongs in partscore with spades as the trump suit. East, therefore, responds 2♠, putting the partnership in the best contract. South passes.

The auction comes back around to West. East's 2♠ response is a signoff bid, setting the contract, so West passes. North also passes and the auction is over. The contract is 2♠ with East as the declarer since East first mentioned spades.

Suggested Opening Lead

South, on declarer's left, makes the opening lead. With a three-card sequence in hearts, South leads the ♥Q, the top of the touching cards. This tells North that South doesn't hold the ♥K but does hold the ♥J and, likely, the ♥10 as well.

Declarer's Plan

South leads the ♥Q and the West hand is placed face up on the table as the dummy. East, as declarer, makes a plan. East's goal is to take at least eight tricks.

East starts by counting the available sure tricks. The partnership has the ♥A–K and the ♦A-K for four winners. Four more tricks are needed.

East browses Declarer's Checklist to develop extra tricks. The spade suit offers the opportunity to promote four winners by driving out the defenders' ♠A and ♠K. The spade suit will provide the extra tricks required.

```
┌─ DECLARER'S PLAN—THE ABC'S ─┐

 Declarer: East      Contract: 2♠

 ASSESS THE SITUATION
   Goal                      8
   Sure Tricks               4
   Extra Tricks Needed       4

 BROWSE DECLARER'S CHECKLIST
   Promotion          4 in spades
   Length
   The Finesse

 CONSIDER THE ORDER
   • Draw trumps first.
   • Develop the extra spade tricks early.
```

After winning the first heart trick, declarer leads a spade, starting to promote winners in the suit by driving out one of the defenders' high cards. South might win the ♠K and lead another heart to drive out dummy's remaining high card. The defenders are also using promotion to develop winners! Declarer leads another spade to drive out North's ♠A. Declarer's remaining spades have all been promoted.

If North leads another heart after winning the ♠A, East can ruff. East can then play one of the established spades winners to draw the defenders' outstanding trump. Declarer can now safely take the two diamond tricks. Declarer finishes with four spade tricks, two heart tricks, and two diamond tricks. That's just enough to make the contract.

DEAL: 8		
DEALER: WEST		

North
- ♠ A Q 9
- ♥ A 6 3
- ♦ 7 6 4 3
- ♣ 9 6 2

NORTH

WEST   EAST

SOUTH

West
- ♠ 8 6 3
- ♥ Q J 10 9
- ♦ Q 10 8
- ♣ Q 7 4

East
- ♠ J 7 5 2
- ♥ 8 5 4
- ♦ J 9
- ♣ K J 10 3

South
- ♠ K 10 4
- ♥ K 7 2
- ♦ A K 5 2
- ♣ A 8 5

Suggested Bidding

WEST	NORTH	EAST	SOUTH
PASS	PASS	PASS	1NT
PASS	3NT	PASS	PASS
PASS			

West is the dealer and has 7 valuation points, all in high cards. That isn't enough to open the bidding, so West passes.

The auction moves to North who has 10 high-card points, not enough to open the bidding. North passes.

East has the next chance to bid and with only 6 high-card points, passes.

South has the last opportunity to open the bidding. With 17 high-card points and a balanced hand, South begins the auction with 1NT.

West passes.

North is the responder to South's 1NT opening bid and has 10 high-card points. North decides **HOW HIGH**. Since South has promised at least 15 valuation points with the 1NT opening bid, there is enough combined strength to try for a game bonus. North decides **WHERE**. With a balanced hand, North chooses a game contract of 3NT.

East, South, and West have nothing more to say and each passes in turn. The auction is over and North-South have contracted for nine tricks with no trump suit. South, having first suggested notrump, is the declarer.

Suggested Opening Lead

West, to declarer's left, makes the opening lead. With a solid sequence in the longest suit, West leads the ♥Q, the top card.

Declarer's Play

After West makes the opening lead, the North hand comes down as the dummy. South is declarer in a contract of 3NT and has to take nine tricks.

South's first step is to assess the situation and count the sure tricks. The partnership has three spade tricks, two heart tricks, two diamond tricks, and a club trick. That's a total of eight. One more trick is required.

┌─── DECLARER'S PLAN—THE ABC'S ───┐

Declarer: South   Contract: 3NT

ASSESS THE SITUATION
Goal	9
Sure Tricks	8
Extra Tricks Needed	1

BROWSE DECLARER'S CHECKLIST
Promotion	
Length	1 in diamonds
The Finesse	

CONSIDER THE ORDER
- Develop the extra diamond trick early.

Going to the second step of the plan, South browses Declarer's Checklist. There are no opportunities to promote an extra winner, but the diamond suit offers the possibility of developing an extra winner through length. There are eight combined diamonds between the North and South hands, leaving five for the defenders. If the missing diamonds are divided 3-2, declarer can create a winner in the suit.

Declarer wins the first heart trick and takes two tricks with the ♦A and ♦K. When both defenders follow suit, there is only one diamond outstanding. Declarer leads a third round of diamonds, giving up a trick to West's ♦Q. West will likely continue by leading another heart, promoting winners in that suit. Declarer can win and lead the last diamond. Declarer wins this trick because the defenders don't have any diamonds left. Declarer takes the remaining winners and has nine tricks. The contract of 3NT is made and North-South receive a game bonus.

Declarer had to give up a diamond trick to the defenders before taking the sure tricks in the other suits. Declarer was then able to regain the lead and take the established diamond trick. If declarer had taken all the winners in the other suits before giving up a diamond trick, declarer would be unable to regain the lead and take advantage of the established diamond winner.

Bridge is the most entertaining and intelligent card game the art of man has so far devised.

—Somerset Maugham

Major Suit Opening Bids and Responses

The 1♥ and 1♠ Opening Bids

If you have enough strength to open the bidding but the hand doesn't meet the requirements for a 1NT opening, the next priority is to decide if the hand qualifies for an opening bid in a major suit, 1♥ or 1♠. Two features are required:

> **OPENING 1♥ OR 1♠**
> 13–21 valuation points
> A five-card or longer suit

With five cards in both hearts and spades, the higher-ranking suit, spades, is opened.

The Strength

The range for an opening bid of 1♥ or 1♠ is much wider than the narrow three-point range for 1NT. It includes hands starting at 13 points, the bottom of the range for opening the bidding at the one level, and goes right up to strong hands of about 21 points. Hands with 22 or more points are opened at the two level, but they are quite rare and are left for a later book in this series (POPULAR CONVENTIONS).

The Length

Although some methods allow an opening bid of 1♥ or 1♠ with a four-card suit, the popular style in North America and throughout most of the world is *five-card majors*. An opening bid of 1♥ or 1♠ promises at least five cards in the suggested trump suit. This will usually help the partnership decide whether the contract should be played with that suit as trumps.

Examples

The following hands have the requirements to open in a major suit, 1♥ or 1♠:

♠ A K 7 5 3
♥ A 6 5
♦ Q 5
♣ 8 6 3

Open 1♠. This hand has 13 high-card points and 1 length point for the fifth spade, bringing the total to 14, enough to open the bidding. Although the hand is balanced, there is not enough strength to open 1NT.

♠ A K Q J
♥ 9 8 6 5 4 2
♦ A 4
♣ 5

Open 1♥. This hand has 14 high-card points plus 2 length points for the six-card suit. Although there are 16 valuation points, the hand is unsuitable for 1NT because it is unbalanced. Choose the longest suit, hearts, even though it is weaker in high-card strength than the spades—"length before strength."

♠ A 8 7 5 4
♥ A K J 6 3
♦ 7 3
♣ 2

Open 1♠. With a choice between five-card suits, open the higher-ranking. The opening bid is the start of a conversation. If partner suggests another trump suit or notrump, you can then mention the heart suit.

These hands do not have the requirements to open in a major suit:

♠ 6 3
♥ Q 8 6 5 3
♦ A 4
♣ K 10 7 3

Pass. Although there is a five-card major suit, the hand has only 9 high-card points plus 1 length point, for a total of 10 valuation points. That isn't enough to open the bidding.

♠ K J 4
♥ K J 8 6 3
♦ A Q
♣ Q 10 5

Open 1NT. This hand has a five-card major suit but is also balanced and falls within the range for a 1NT opening bid. There are 16 high-card points plus 1 length point for the five-card suit. 1NT takes priority.

♠ K 4
♥ A Q 7 5
♦ 8 3
♣ A 9 7 6 2

Open 1♣. There are 13 high-card points plus 1 length point for the five-card club suit. With no five-card major suit, open in the longer minor suit.

Responding to Opening Bids of 1♥ or 1♠

An opening 1♥ or 1♠ bid is much less specific about opener's strength and distribution than an opening bid of 1NT. As a result, the approach to responding is different. Responder can't decide **How High** and **Where** to play the contract with one bid because responder needs more information: opener could have as few as 13 or as many as 21 points; opener could have a balanced hand or a very unbalanced hand. There are no sign-off bids by responder after a major suit opening. There are only invitational and forcing bids.

Responder's Priority – Showing Support – Invitational

Since opener has suggested playing with a major suit as trumps, responder's priority is to give an opinion on the suggested suit. If responder likes the trump suit, responder usually lets partner know right away by *showing support*. This invites opener to bid again or pass.

To raise or support partner's major suit opening, responder
has to have at least three cards in the suit.

The opening 1♥ or 1♠ bid shows a five-card suit or longer. If
responder has three or more cards in the suit, the combined number of cards is at least eight, enough to be comfortable with that
suit as trumps.

In addition to showing support for opener's suit, responder helps
opener determine the combined strength of the partnership hands
by describing the strength of responder's hand. This is done by
raising opener's suit to the appropriate level using the following
guideline:

RAISING OPENER'S MAJOR SUIT

RESPONDER'S
VALUATION POINTS

0–5 points	Pass. Game is unlikely; stay low and stop in partscore.
6–10 points	Raise to the two level. A game bonus is possible if opener has some extra strength.
11–12 points	Raise to the three level.* A game bonus is likely if opener has more than 13 or 14 points.
13+ points	Get to game. The partnership has 26 or more combined valuation points, enough for the game bonus.

*It's preferable to have at least four-card support to raise to the three or four level.

The general idea is that the more strength responder has, the
higher responder raises. Opener can then decide if the partnership
belongs in partscore, game, or even slam.

Dummy Points

Once the partnership has found an eight-card or longer major suit fit, short suits can become valuable. A void, for example, can be more powerful than an ace. If the defenders lead the ace of a suit in which dummy has no cards, declarer can trump the ace in the dummy and win the trick. Declarer may even be able to trump more than one of the defenders' winners. To take this into account, the distribution of the hand is valued using *dummy points* in place of length points when a player is going to be the dummy. If you plan to raise partner's major suit, you'll be the dummy.

DUMMY POINTS	
Void	5 points
Singleton	3 points
Doubleton	1 point

Examples of Raising Opener's Major Suit—Invitational

Here are examples when responder agrees with opener's trump suit.

Your partner opens 1♠ ◀——— 13–21 points; a five-card or longer suit

♠ J 8 6 3
♥ 5 2
♦ J 8 7 4
♣ 10 9 3

Pass. You have support for partner's major suit, but there are only 2 high-card points plus 1 dummy point for the doubleton heart. Game is unlikely even if opener has 21 points.

♠ K 10 5
♥ 7 4 3 2
♦ 8 4
♣ K Q 7 2

2♠. With three-card support, there is a guaranteed eight-card trump fit, since opener has promised at least five. You have 8 high-card points plus 1 dummy point for the doubleton diamond. Raise to the two level, showing support and about 6-10 valuation points. Opener can then decide whether to stop in partscore or try for the game bonus.

| Your partner opens 1♠ | ◄——— 13–21 points; a five-card or longer suit |

♠ Q 10 5 4
♥ Q 9 6 2
♦ 7
♣ A 8 5 4

3♠. You have four-card support for partner's major suit. Since you are planning to raise, value the hand using dummy points. There are 8 high-card points plus 3 dummy points for the singleton diamond. That's enough to make a jump raise to the three level. This is highly invitational to a game contract. Opener will only pass with a bare minimum opening bid of 13 or 14 points.

♠ A Q J 5 4
♥ –
♦ Q 9 8 5
♣ 7 6 4 3

4♠. There are only 9 high-card points but you can add 5 dummy points for the heart void for a total of 14 valuation points. That's enough to take the partnership directly to the game bonus level[16].

Responder's Second Choice—A New Suit—Forcing

If responder doesn't have a fit for opener's major, the next priority is to look for another possible trump suit. There is a limitation, however. The partnership doesn't want to get too high on the Bidding Ladder while searching for a trump suit if it doesn't have enough combined strength to take the required tricks.

Since opener has promised 13 or more points, responder needs about 6 or more points to bid a *new suit* at the one level and have reasonable assurance that the partnership has at least half the overall strength on the deal. To introduce a new suit at the two level, responder needs about 11 or more points[17] to be reasonably confident that the partnership can take eight or more tricks. This is different from the response of a new suit at the two level after an opening bid of 1NT, which can be done with a very weak hand.

[16] There are other methods to get to the game level in a major suit, but they are beyond the scope of this text.

[17] Some partnerships drop this requirement to as few as 10 points but the modern style is in the opposite direction. It is becoming popular in some auctions to require at least 13 points to introduce a new suit at the two level, a two-over-one response.

Opener needs a five-card or longer suit to open 1♥ or 1♠. Responder can suggest a different trump suit, however, with only a four-card or longer suit. There is an exception. A response of 2♥ after a 1♠ opening promises a five-card or longer suit.

In summary, here are responder's guidelines for bidding a new suit:

RESPONDING IN A NEW SUIT

At the One Level

- 6 or more points.
- A four-card or longer suit.

At the Two Level

- 11 or more points*.
- A four-card or longer suit to respond 2♣ or 2♦.
- A five-card or longer suit to respond 2♥.

*13 or more in some methods.

A response in a new suit is forcing. Opener is expected to make another bid.

Examples of Responding in a New Suit—Forcing

| Your partner opens 1♥ | ◀—— 13–21 points; a five-card or longer suit |

♠ Q J 7 5
♥ 6 2
♦ A J 8 3
♣ 6 5 2

1♠. You don't have support for partner's hearts but have 8 valuation points, enough to respond. You need only a four-card suit to suggest spades as a trump suit at the one level. The 1♠ response, a new suit at the one level, promises 6 or more points and four or more spades. It's forcing and opener has to bid again.

> Your partner opens 1♥ ◄———— 13–21 points; a five-card or longer suit

♠ A K J 8 5
♥ 4
♦ K Q 4
♣ J 8 6 3

1♠. The response of a new suit at the one level shows 6 or more points. This hand is worth 14 high-card points plus 1 length point for the five-card suit. You don't need to go to the two level to show the spade suit. A response of 1♠ is forcing and opener will bid again. You can show the extra strength on your next bid.

♠ A 9 5
♥ 5 3
♦ A Q J 8 7
♣ Q 8 2

2♦. This hand is worth 14 valuation points, 13 high-card points plus 1 length point for the five-card suit. That's enough to bid a new suit at the two level and suggest diamonds as the trump suit, since you don't have support for hearts. Opener will bid again.

Choice of Suits

With a choice of four-card or longer suits, responder bids the longest unless it would have to be at the two level and responder doesn't have the required strength. With a choice among suits of equal length, use the following guideline:

RESPONDER'S CHOICE OF SUITS

- With a choice of four-card suits, bid the cheapest, the one that comes next on the Bidding Ladder.
- With a choice of five-card suits, bid the higher-ranking.

Here are some examples after partner opens 1♠.

| Your partner opens 1♠ | ◄─── 13–21 points; a five-card or longer suit |

♠ 5
♥ K J 7 2
♦ A J 8 6 5
♣ K 8 2

2♦. With enough strength to bid a new suit at the two level, choose the longest suit, diamonds.

♠ 7 4
♥ A Q 8 5 3
♦ 7
♣ A K J 8 5

2♥. With a choice between two five-card suits, bid the higher-ranking, hearts.

♠ Q 2
♥ 8 6 3
♦ A K 7 4
♣ K J 6 3

2♣. With enough to make a bid at the two level and a choice of four-card suits, choose the one that comes next going up the Bidding Ladder. 2♣ comes before 2♦.

Responder's Third Choice—1NT—Invitational

| Your partner opens 1♥ | ◄─── 13–21 points; a five-card or longer suit |

If responder has 6 or more points but can't support partner's major, can't bid a new suit at the one level, and doesn't have enough strength to bid a new suit at the two level, the only choice remaining is to respond 1NT[18]. For example:

♠ K 8 4
♥ 6 2
♦ Q 9 7 4
♣ A 10 6 5

1NT. You don't have support for opener's heart suit and you don't have a four-card suit that can be bid at the one level. With 9 valuation points, you have enough to respond but don't

---

[18] The range of the 1NT response depends on the partnership agreement. If the partnership has agreed that a new suit response at the two level promises at least 11 points, then the range for a 1NT response is 6–10; if the partnership has agreed that a new suit response at the two level promises at least 13 points, the range for a 1NT response is 6–12.

have enough to bid a new suit at the two level. 1NT is the only choice remaining.

♠ J 8 3
♥ 7
♦ K 8 6 5 3 2
♣ Q 7 4

1NT. The 1NT response doesn't promise a balanced hand. It sends the message to opener that you have 6 or more points but not enough strength to bid a new suit at the two level. It also says you can't support partner's suit and don't have a four-card or longer suit that can be bid at the one level.

Opener's Rebid

Unless everyone passes after the opening bid, opener will have a second chance to bid and further describe the strength and distribution of the hand. Opener's second bid is referred to as *opener's rebid*.

Opener's choice of rebid depends on whether responder:

- Raised opener's major.
- Bid a new suit.
- Bid notrump.

Let's look at each situation in turn.

Opener's Rebid After Responder Raised Opener's Major

When responder raises opener's major suit, the trump suit has been agreed. WHERE has been decided. It is only a question of How HIGH the partnership belongs: partscore, game, or slam. Opener adds up the combined strength and decides whether to pass, move toward the bonus level, or go right to the bonus level.

Here are examples after responder makes a simple raise to the two level, showing support and about 6–10 points.

OPENER (YOU)	RESPONDER (PARTNER)

13–21 points; a five-card or longer suit	→ 1♥ ?	2♥ ← 6–10 points; heart support

♠ J 6 4
♥ A 8 7 6 5
♦ K 7 3
♣ A J

Pass. You have 14 valuation points: 13 high-card points plus 1 length point for the five-card suit. Even if responder has 10 points, there is not enough combined strength to go for the bonus level. You have found a trump fit. Settle for partscore by passing.

♠ A 8
♥ K J 9 7 6 3
♦ A Q 5
♣ J 6

3♥. This hand has 15 high-card points and 2 length points for the six-card suit for a total of 17. If responder has the top of the range for the response, 9 or 10 points, a game bonus should be possible. Move toward the bonus level by rebidding 3♥. If partner has the bottom of the range, 6 or 7 points, the partnership can still stop in partscore.

♠ A 10 8
♥ A Q J 8 6 3
♦ A K
♣ 7 2

4♥. This hand is worth 20 valuation points: 18 high-card points plus 2 length points for the six-card suit. Even if partner has only 6 points, there should be enough combined strength to go for the game bonus. Jump right to the game level.

Here are some examples after responder makes an invitational jump raise to the three level, showing support and about 11-12 points.

OPENER (YOU)　　　　RESPONDER (PARTNER)

| 13–21 points; a five-card or longer suit | ➤ | 1♥ ? | | 3♥ | ◄ | 11–12 points; heart support |

♠ K J
♥ Q J 8 7 4
♦ K Q
♣ 8 6 5 2

Pass. You have 13 valuation points: 12 high-card points plus 1 length point for the five-card suit. With a bare minimum for the opening bid, the partnership is unlikely to have the combined strength for the game bonus. Pass and settle for partscore.

♠ K Q
♥ Q 9 7 6 4 2
♦ A Q 8 3
♣ 5

4♥. This hand has 13 high-card points and 2 length points for the six-card suit for a total of 15. Since responder is showing 11 or 12 points, there should be enough combined strength to make 10 tricks. Accept the invitation and go for the bonus.

If responder has enough strength to take the partnership to the game bonus level, opener won't need to consider bidding any higher unless there is the possibility of a slam bonus. A discussion of slam bidding is outside the current scope.

Opener's Rebid After Responder Bids a New Suit

When responder bids a new suit, the partnership has not yet agreed on a trump suit. Even if opener likes responder's choice of trump suit, opener can't pass because responder's strength is unlimited. A new suit response is forcing, so opener must make a rebid that paints a clear picture of opener's distribution and strength.

Opener considers the type of bid that best describes the distribution. With support for responder's suggested trump suit, opener can raise to show the fit. If opener can't support responder's suit, opener can suggest another trump suit, or rebid the original suit with extra length, or bid notrump to show a balanced hand.

At the same time, opener wants to clarify the strength of the hand because the opening bid covered a wide range of about 13–21 points. As a guideline, opener puts the hand in one of three ranges:

13–16 points	Minimum strength opening hand
17–18 points	Medium strength opening hand
19–21 points	Maximum strength opening hand

With a minimum hand, opener rebids as cheaply as possible, showing no extra strength. With a medium hand, opener will often jump a level to show the extra strength. With a maximum hand, opener will make sure the partnership reaches at least a game bonus level. Even if responder has as few as 6 points, the partnership should have enough combined strength for game.

When determining the strength of the hand for the rebid, opener can value the hand using dummy points if planning to support responder's suit.

Here are examples when responder bids a new suit at the one level and opener has support for responder's suit.

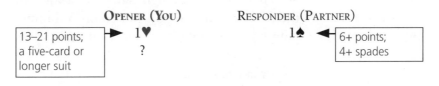

OPENER (YOU)	RESPONDER (PARTNER)
13–21 points; a five-card or longer suit → 1♥ ?	1♠ ← 6+ points; 4+ spades

♠ K J 6 4
♥ A J 7 6 5
♦ K 4
♣ 7 2

2♠. You have support for spades. You can't pass, however, since the partnership may have enough combined strength to go for a bonus. Since you are planning to raise partner's suit,

♠ K J 6 4
♥ A J 7 6 5
♦ K 4
♣ 7 2

revalue the hand using dummy points. Your hand will be the dummy if the contract is played with spades as the trump suit. You have 12 high-card points plus 1 dummy point for each doubleton. The total of 14 points leaves the hand in the minimum strength category, so make cheapest descriptive rebid by raising to the two level.

♠ A Q 8 2
♥ K Q J 8 6
♦ 3
♣ Q 7 5

3♠. When valuing the hand as an opening bid, count 14 high-card points and 1 length point, for a total of 15. When responder bids 1♠, however, the hand becomes more valuable. You have found a trump fit, and the singleton diamond should be valuable in preventing the defenders from taking tricks in the suit. The hand is now worth 17 valuation points: 14 high-card points plus 3 dummy points for the singleton diamond. That puts it in the medium strength category and you can show the extra strength by jumping to 3♠ instead of making the minimum raise to 2♠. If responder has only 6 or 7 points, the partnership can stop in partscore. With more, responder can accept the invitation and go for the bonus.

♠ A J 8 2
♥ A K 9 7 3
♦ K 9 6 2
♣ –

4♠. There are only 15 high-card points, but with the fit with partner, you can count 5 dummy points for the void in clubs. That makes this a maximum-strength hand of 20 points. Since responder has at least 6 points, take the partnership right to the bonus level in spades.

Here are examples when responder bids a new suit at the one level and opener doesn't have support for responder's suit.

OPENER (YOU)   RESPONDER (PARTNER)

13–21 points; a five-card or longer suit → 1♥   1♠ ← 6+ points; 4+ spades

?

♠ 6 3
♥ K J 8 5 4
♦ K J 3
♣ A J 7

1NT. You have 13 high-card points plus 1 length point for the five-card suit. You don't have support for responder's suit. Having already shown a five-card heart suit, you can finish the description by showing a balanced hand. With a minimum-strength opening, bid notrump as cheaply as possible.

♠ 7
♥ A K J 8 4
♦ 6 5 2
♣ K Q J 7

2♣. Responder didn't show support for hearts and you don't have support for spades. Having already promised a five-card heart suit, suggest a second suit as trumps. This tells partner you have an unbalanced hand with at least five hearts and at least four clubs.

♠ K Q
♥ A Q 10 9 7 5
♦ 6 2
♣ 9 8 4

2♥. Responder may have only a four-card suit. You need at least three, and preferably four, spades to show support. Since you can't support partner's suit and you don't have a balanced hand or a second suit to show, rebid the heart suit, showing the extra length in that suit.

♠ K J
♥ A K J 10 7 5 3
♦ 4
♣ Q J 4

3♥. This is similar to the previous hand except that you have a medium strength hand. You have 15 high-card points plus 3 length points for the seven-card suit. Show the extra strength by jumping a level. With only 6 or 7 points, responder can pass and the partnership will rest in partscore. With a little more, responder can accept the invitation and bid to a bonus level.

Opener's Rebid After Responder Bids 1NT

A response of 1NT shows a hand with 6 or more points but not enough to bid a new suit at the two level. Responder doesn't have support for opener's suit or a four-card or longer suit that can be bid at the one level. Opener can take all this into account when choosing a rebid.

Here are examples after you open 1♠ and partner responds 1NT.

	OPENER (YOU)	RESPONDER (PARTNER)	
13–21 points; a five-card or longer suit	► 1♠ ?	1NT ◄	6–10+ points;

♠ A J 8 7 5
♥ Q 4
♦ K Q 9 6 2
♣ 2

2♦. Partner doesn't have support for spades, so suggest another trump suit by bidding your second suit. You are expecting partner to choose between spades and diamonds, although partner has other choices. For example, partner might have a long heart suit but not enough strength to bid it at the two level. Partner could show the heart suit after your 2♦ bid, having already limited the strength with the 1NT response.

♠ Q J 10 8 7 6
♥ 4
♦ A K J
♣ 7 5 3

2♠. Although responder doesn't have three-card or longer support for spades, the partnership could still have an eight-card fit if responder has a doubleton spade. Even if responder has a singleton spade, spades will likely be the best trump suit. With a minimum-strength opening bid, rebid the spades at the cheapest available level.

♠ K Q 10 8 3
♥ J 7 5
♦ A J
♣ Q 9 4

Pass[19]. You have a minimum-strength balanced hand and have already told partner about the five-card spade suit. Responder's strength is limited so the game level appears out of reach. 1NT looks to be the best contract, so you can pass and stop in partscore.

Responder's Rebid

By the time it comes to *responder's rebid*, responder should have a good description of opener's strength and distribution. Responder should be able to decide **How High** and **Where**. For example:

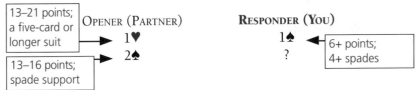

13–21 points; a five-card or longer suit	OPENER (PARTNER)		RESPONDER (YOU)	
	1♥		1♠	6+ points; 4+ spades
13–16 points; spade support	2♠		?	

♠ K J 8 7
♥ 8 2
♦ Q 8 4
♣ J 9 7 5

Pass. Opener has shown support for your spade suit and described a minimum-strength opening bid by raising to the cheapest level. Since you have 7 high-card points and opener has a minimum opening with at most 16 points, you know **How High**, partscore. You now also know **Where** the partnership belongs, spades. The partnership has found its best contract.

♠ A Q 9 7 2
♥ K 4
♦ A 4
♣ 9 7 4 2

4♠. Your hand is worth 13 high-card points plus 1 length point for the five-card suit. Partner has at least 13 points for the opening bid, so you know **How High**. The partnership belongs at the game bonus level. Partner has supported your suggested trump suit, so you also know **Where**. Go to the bonus level in the agreed suit.

[19] Some partnerships treat a 1NT response to a major suit as forcing and opener must bid again. Although this approach is becoming more popular, it is outside the current scope.

♠ K 10 9 7 4 2
♥ 5 3
♦ Q 8 5
♣ A 4

3♠. You have 9 high-card points plus 2 length points for a total of 11. Opener has shown a minimum-strength hand and could have as few as 13 points or as many as 16. To decide **How High**, move toward the game level. The partnership can still stop in partscore if opener has 13 or 14 points. If opener has a little extra, the partnership will reach the bonus level. Once partner raises your suit you have found a suitable trump fit, so you know **Where**.

Declarer's Plan—The ABC's

Assess the Situation

- Goal
- Sure Tricks
- Extra Tricks Needed

When there are already enough sure tricks, declarer goes ahead and takes them. If there are not enough sure tricks, declarer moves to the second step of the plan.

Browse Declarer's Checklist to Develop Extra Tricks

There are advantages to playing with a trump suit. The trumps can be used to stop the defenders from taking their winners in a suit because you can ruff with a trump once you have no cards left in the suit. So, in addition to the three ways for developing extra tricks that can be used in both notrump and suit contracts, a fourth way can be added in suit contracts:

- Promotion
- Length
- The Finesse
- Trumping in dummy

DUMMY
♠ 9 7 3
♥ 2

DECLARER
♠ A K Q J 10
♥ A 3

Suppose the trump suit is spades and these are the combined spade and heart holdings between declarer and dummy.

If declarer takes all five spade winners and then the ♥A, declarer gets six tricks. If declarer plays the ♥A and then leads the ♥3 and ruffs it in the dummy, declarer gets seven tricks, the ♥A, the ruff, and the five spade winners in declarer's hand. Declarer gains a trick by ruffing in the dummy.

If declarer has the greater length in the trump suit, which is usually the case, there is no advantage in ruffing in declarer's hand. Suppose spades are the trump suit and these are the combined spade and heart holdings.

DUMMY
♠ 9 7 3
♥ A 3

DECLARER
♠ A K Q J 10
♥ 2

Declarer has six tricks, five spade winners and the ♥A. If declarer plays the ♥A and leads the ♥3 and trumps it, there are still only six tricks. Nothing is gained.

To recognize the opportunity to ruff in dummy, look for side suits (non trump suits) that have more cards in declarer's hand than in the dummy. Here are two examples when spades are trumps.

DUMMY
♦ 7 3

DECLARER
♦ A K 4

Declarer has two winners in this suit. After winning tricks with the ♦A and ♦K, declarer can get a third trick by leading the ♦4 and ruffing with one of dummy's trumps.

DUMMY
♣ 8

DECLARER
♣ 7 2

Declarer has no winners in this suit. If declarer leads a club and gives up a trick to the defenders, dummy will now be void in clubs. On regaining the lead, declarer can lead the remaining club and ruff in dummy to get a trick.

Consider the Order

When it comes to the third stage of the plan, considering the order in which to play the cards, here is an important tip:

Keep enough trumps in dummy. If you are planning on ruffing in dummy, you can't afford to play so many rounds of trumps that there are no trumps left when you want to ruff. Sometimes you may have to delay drawing trumps until you are finished ruffing in dummy. Also, keep in mind that the defenders may lead trumps to try and prevent you from ruffing in the dummy.

Defense – Getting a Ruff

The defenders can sometimes use the trump suit against declarer. They have to work together to ruff declarer's winners.

For example, suppose East and West are defending and the trump suit is spades. This is the layout of the heart suit with West on lead.

West leads the ♥A, top of the touching high cards against a suit contract. The ♥A wins the trick. If West continues with the ♥K and leads the suit a third time, East can ruff dummy's ♥Q with a low trump and the defenders will get three tricks.

	DUMMY	
	♥ Q J 3	
WEST		EAST
♥ A K 7 5 4		♥ 9 2
	DECLARER	
	♥ 10 8 6	

How does West know to lead the suit a third time? East can use an attitude signal (see page 54). On the first trick, East plays the ♥9, an encouraging card. When West continues the suit, East follows with the ♥2. The "high-low" in hearts encourages West to lead the suit a third time and East gets to ruff.

With three low hearts, East would play the ♥2 on the first trick, a discouraging signal. Now West would know to look elsewhere for tricks for the defense.

SUMMARY

Opening 1♥ or 1♠

- 13–21 valuation points.
- A five-card or longer suit
- With a choice of five-card suits, bid the higher-ranking.

Responses to 1♥ or 1♠

Responder's priorities:
- Raise opener's suit with support.
- Bid a new suit.
- Bid notrump.

RAISING OPENER'S MAJOR SUIT

0–5 points	Pass. Game is unlikely; stay low and stop in partscore.
6–10 points	Raise to the two level. A game bonus is possible if opener has some extra strength.
11–12 points	Raise to the three level. A game bonus is likely if opener has more than 13 or 14 points.
13+ points	Get to game. The partnership has 26 or more combined valuation points, enough for the game bonus.

BIDDING LADDER

Level	Bids	Bonus Level (Combined Valuation Pts.)
	7NT	
7-Level (13 Tricks)	7♠ 7♥ 7♦ 7♣	GRAND SLAM 37+
	6NT	
6-Level (12 Tricks)	6♠ 6♥ 6♦ 6♣	SMALL SLAM 33+
	5NT	
5-Level (11 Tricks)	5♠ 5♥ 5♦ 5♣	GAME 29+ PTS.
	4NT	
4-Level (10 Tricks)	4♠ 4♥ 4♦ 4♣	GAME 26+ PTS.
	3NT	
3-Level (9 Tricks)	3♠ 3♥ 3♦ 3♣	GAME 25+ PTS.
	2NT	
2-Level (8 Tricks)	2♠ 2♥ 2♦ 2♣	
	1NT	
1-Level (7 Tricks)	1♠ 1♥ 1♦ 1♣	

When planning to raise opener's major suit, responder can value the hand using dummy points in place of length points:

DUMMY POINTS

Void	5 points
Singleton	3 points
Doubleton	1 point

RESPONDING IN A NEW SUIT

At the One Level:
- 6 or more points
- A four-card or longer suit.

At the Two Level:
- 11 or more points.
- A four-card or longer suit to respond 2♣ or 2♦.
- A five-card or longer suit to respond 2♥.

If responder has a choice of suits to bid:
- With a choice of four-card suits, bid the cheapest (the one that comes next on the Bidding Ladder).
- With a choice of five-card suits, bid the higher-ranking.

RESPONDING 1NT
- 6–10 points (some partnerships use a higher upper range).
- No support for opener's suit.
- No four-card or longer suit that can be bid at the one level.

Opener's Rebid

Opener chooses a rebid keeping in mind that a response in a new suit is forcing. As a general guideline, the more strength opener has, the more opener bids.

The following classification can be used to help opener decide how high to bid after a response at the one level:

13 – 16 points	Minimum-strength opening bid.
17 – 18 points	Medium-strength opening bid.
19 – 21 points	Maximum-strength opening bid.

Responder's Rebid

By the time responder makes a rebid, opener has had two bids to describe the hand. At this point, responder asks How High and Where and places the contract.

Declarer's Plan—The ABCs

Assess the Situation
- Goal
- Sure Tricks
- Extra Tricks Needed

Browse Declarer's Checklist if Extra Tricks are Required
- Promotion
- Length
- The Finesse
- Trumping in dummy

Consider the Order
- Keep enough trumps in dummy when planning to get extra tricks through trumping.

Quiz – Part I

You are the dealer. What call would you make with the following hands?

a) ♠ Q 10 7 6 4
  ♥ A K
  ♦ K 9 6 3
  ♣ 8 4

b) ♠ A Q
  ♥ K 10 9 7 4
  ♦ A
  ♣ A Q 8 6 3

c) ♠ 4
  ♥ A Q J 7
  ♦ K J 8 6 3
  ♣ K 8 2

Partner opens the bidding 1♥.

OPENER (PARTNER)	RESPONDER (YOU)
1♥	?

13–21 points; a five-card or longer suit

What would you respond with each of the following hands?

d) ♠ J 6 3
  ♥ 7 4 3
  ♦ Q 8 6 4
  ♣ 9 8 2

e) ♠ 7 2
  ♥ K J 4
  ♦ K 8 6 4
  ♣ 10 8 6 2

f) ♠ A 4
  ♥ Q 10 7 3
  ♦ A 9 6 5
  ♣ 10 8 2

g) ♠ 8 5 2
  ♥ A K J 8 6
  ♦ 3
  ♣ Q 10 9 5

h) ♠ K 10 8 6
  ♥ 4 2
  ♦ K Q 8 3
  ♣ 7 6 4

i) ♠ 6
  ♥ Q 5
  ♦ K 6 4 3
  ♣ A Q J 8 4 2

j) ♠ Q 10 8 5 3
  ♥ 7
  ♦ A K J 8 4
  ♣ 6 3

k) ♠ 9 4 2
  ♥ A Q
  ♦ K J 7 2
  ♣ Q J 8 3

l) ♠ K 8 3
  ♥ 9 7
  ♦ Q 10 7 5
  ♣ K J 7 4

m) ♠ Q 6 4
  ♥ 5
  ♦ K J 7 6 3 2
  ♣ J 8 5

n) ♠ Q J 7 4
  ♥ 8 3
  ♦ 8 4
  ♣ K 9 8 6 5

o) ♠ J 6 3
  ♥ 4
  ♦ J 9 8 6 5
  ♣ 8 6 4 2

Answers to Quiz — Part I

a) **1♠**. The hand has 12 high-card points and 1 length point for the five-card suit. With a five-card major suit, open 1♠.

b) **1♥**. This hand has 19 high-card points plus 1 length point for each five-card suit for a total of 21. With a choice between five-card suits, open the higher-ranking, hearts.

c) **1♦**. There are 14 high-card points plus 1 length point. The hand is unbalanced and there is no five-card major. Open 1♦.

d) **Pass**. With fewer than 6 points, leave the partnership in partscore.

e) **2♥**. You have three-card support. Valuing with dummy points, there are 7 high-card points plus 1 dummy point for the doubleton spade. The total of 8 is enough to raise to the two level.

f) **3♥**. There are 10 high-card points plus 1 dummy point for the doubleton spade. Make a highly invitational jump raise to 3♥ showing the support and 11–12 points.

g) **4♥**. There are 10 high-card points and you can add 3 dummy points for the singleton diamond. That's enough to take the partnership to the game level.

h) **1♠**. You have 8 high-card points but don't have three-card support for opener's suit. Bid a new suit at the one level, showing four or more spades and 6 or more points.

i) **2♣**. With 12 high-card points plus 2 length points, you have enough strength to bid a new suit at the two level. With a choice of suits, bid the longest.

j) **1♠**. With a choice of five-card suits, bid the higher-ranking, spades.

k) **2♣**. With 13 high-card points but fewer than three hearts, respond in a new suit. With a choice of four-card suits, bid the cheapest.

l) **1NT**. With only 9 high-card points you aren't strong enough to introduce a new suit at the two level. Instead, respond 1NT.

m) **1NT**. The 1NT response doesn't promise a balanced hand.

n) **1♠**. Although the clubs are longer than the spades, you don't have enough strength to bid a new suit at the two level. You do have enough strength to bid a new suit at the one level.

o) **Pass**. Although you don't like partner's choice of trump suit, bidding any more is likely to get your side much too high.

Quiz – Part II

You open the bidding 1♠ and partner raises to 2♠.

OPENER (YOU)	RESPONDER (PARTNER)
13–21 points; a five-card or longer suit ▶ 1♠ ?	2♠ ◀ 6–10 points; spade support

What do you rebid with each of the following hands?

a) ♠ K J 9 7 2
   ♥ A Q 5
   ♦ 6
   ♣ Q 9 7 3

b) ♠ A Q 9 8 7 5
   ♥ A Q
   ♦ 6 4
   ♣ K 8 5

c) ♠ A J 10 8 6
   ♥ A Q
   ♦ A K J 2
   ♣ 9 6

You open the bidding 1♥ and partner responds 2♣.

OPENER (YOU)	RESPONDER (PARTNER)
13–21 points; a five-card or longer suit ▶ 1♥ ?	2♣ ◀ 11+ points; a four-card or longer suit

What do you rebid with each of the following hands?

d) ♠ 7 5
   ♥ K J 9 8 7 5
   ♦ A J 4
   ♣ Q 3

e) ♠ K Q
   ♥ A 9 8 6 3
   ♦ 8 5
   ♣ K J 6 2

f) ♠ A J 9
   ♥ Q J 7 6 3
   ♦ K Q 7
   ♣ 10 3

You open the bidding 1♥ and partner responds 1NT.

OPENER (YOU)	RESPONDER (PARTNER)
13–21 points; a five-card or longer suit ▶ 1♥ ?	1NT ◀ 6–10+ points

What do you rebid with each of the following hands?

g) ♠ A 4
   ♥ K Q 8 7 5
   ♦ Q J 8 5 3
   ♣ 4

h) ♠ 5
   ♥ A K J 10 8 5 3
   ♦ A K
   ♣ Q 6 2

i) ♠ K Q 9
   ♥ A Q J 8 4
   ♦ K 7
   ♣ Q 10 4

Answers to Quiz — Part II

a) **Pass**. You have 13 valuation points: 12 high-card points and 1 length point for the five-card suit. Responder's raise to the two level shows three-card or longer support and 6–10 points. The partnership has found a suitable trump fit and doesn't have the combined strength for a game bonus. Stop in partscore.

b) **3♠**. Partner has promised 6-10 points and you have 17 valuation points: 15 high-card points plus 2 length points for the six-card suit. Move toward game, leaving the final decision to responder.

c) **4♠**. This hand has 19 high-card points plus 1 length point for a total of 20 valuation points. Even if responder has only 6 points, the partnership belongs at the game bonus level.

d) **2♥**. Responder's bid in a new suit is forcing, so you can't pass even with a minimum. Rebid your suit at the cheapest level to show the minimum-strength opening bid and the extra length.

e) **3♣**. Responder hasn't shown support for your suggested trump suit, but you have support for responder's suit. Let partner know the partnership has a fit by raising to the three level. You can't pass, even with a minimum opening bid.

f) **2NT**. Responder's bid is forcing, so make the most descriptive rebid. With a balanced hand, rebid in notrump at the cheapest available level, showing a minimum opening bid.

g) **2♦**. Partner didn't like your first suggestion for a trump suit but has at least 6 points. Show the second suit and see which trump suit partner prefers.

h) **4♥**. You have 17 high-card points plus 3 length points for the seven-card suit. Since responder has at least 6 points, the partnership has the combined strength for a game contract. Although partner didn't support your heart suit, you don't need support for hearts to be a suitable trump suit. Bid to the game.

i) **2NT**. You have a balanced hand with 17 high-card points plus 1 length point. The total of 18 points was too much to open 1NT, so you opened in the five-card major suit. Partner has 6–10 points. Invite partner to continue to game by raising to 2NT.

Quiz – Part III

Partner opens 1♥ and you raise to 2♥. Partner now rebids 3♥.

13–21 points; a five-card or longer suit	OPENER (PARTNER)	RESPONDER (YOU)	
	1♥	2♥	6–10 points; heart support
17–18 points; invitational	3♥	?	

What call do you make with each of the following hands when the auction returns to you?

a) ♠ 9 7 2
   ♥ Q J 5
   ♦ 8 7 3
   ♣ K 10 9 5

b) ♠ Q 2
   ♥ 10 8 5 3
   ♦ A Q 6 2
   ♣ J 3 2

c) ♠ A J 6
   ♥ Q 10 6 2
   ♦ 8 5 4
   ♣ J 10 7

If spades are trumps, do the following side suits provide an opportunity to trump in the dummy?

d) DUMMY
   ♣ 9

   DECLARER
   ♣ 6 4

e) DUMMY
   ♥ 5

   DECLARER
   ♥ A 8 5

f) DUMMY
   ♦ 9 7 5

   DECLARER
   ♦ 6

g) DUMMY
   ♣ K 4

   DECLARER
   ♣ A 6 3

East and West are defending against a spade contract and this is the layout of the diamond suit. How can the defenders get three tricks?

                    DUMMY
                    ♦ Q 7 3
        WEST   EAST
     ♦ A K 8 6 5   ♦ 10 2
                  DECLARER
                  ♦ J 9 4

Answers to Quiz — Part III

a) **Pass**. Opener's rebid of 3♥ shows a medium-strength opening bid of about 17 or 18 points. With less, opener would have passed. Opener's bid is inviting you to continue to the game bonus level. With only 6 high-card points, reject opener's invitation by passing to stop in partscore.

b) **4♥**. With 9 high-card points plus 1 dummy point for the doubleton spade, you are at the top of the range for your raise to 2♥. Accept opener's invitation and go for the game bonus.

c) **4♥/Pass**. With 8 points you are on the borderline between passing and accepting. There is no right or wrong, it's simply a close decision. You might be influenced by your four-card support and extra 10's to accept and go for the bonus.

d) **Yes**. If declarer gives up one club trick to the defenders, dummy will be void in clubs. Declarer can later lead the remaining club and ruff in dummy, assuming there is still a trump left in the dummy.

e) **Yes**. Declarer has an opportunity to ruff two hearts in dummy. After taking a trick with the ♥A, declarer can lead a heart and trump it in dummy with a spade. Later, declarer can lead the remaining heart and also trump it in dummy.

f) **No**. There are more diamonds in the dummy than in declarer's hand. Declarer won't be able to ruff a diamond in the dummy. Ruffing a diamond in declarer's hand is unlikely to gain a trick.

g) **Yes**. Declarer can start by playing the ♣K, high card from the short side. Then the ♣4 can be played to declarer's ♣A. Declarer's third club can then be led and ruffed in the dummy.

h) After West wins the first two tricks with the ♦A and ♦K, West can lead a third round for East to trump. East can help by giving West an encouraging signal with the ♦10 on the first round of the suit.

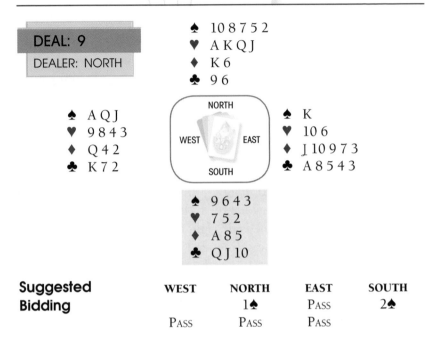

	♠ 108752
	♥ AKQJ
	♦ K6
	♣ 96

| **DEAL: 9** |
| DEALER: NORTH |

♠ AQJ
♥ 9843
♦ Q42
♣ K72

♠ K
♥ 106
♦ J10973
♣ A8543

♠ 9643
♥ 752
♦ A85
♣ QJ10

Suggested Bidding

WEST	NORTH	EAST	SOUTH
	1♠	Pass	2♠
Pass	Pass	Pass	

North has 13 high-card points and 1 length point for the five-card spade suit and starts with 1♠, the five-card major suit. Although the heart suit has more strength, North can't open 1♥ because that would promise a five-card or longer suit.

East has 10 valuation points: 8 high-card points plus 1 length point for each five-card suit. That isn't enough to enter the auction.

South has 7 high-card points and support for partner's major suit. South responds 2♠, showing the support and about 6–10 points.

West has 12 high-card points but that isn't enough to enter the auction, especially since West would have to bid at the three level to suggest a trump suit.

North knows South has at most 10 points for the raise to the two level and could have as few as 6. Since North has 14 points, the partnership doesn't have enough combined strength to go for a game bonus. North settles for partscore by passing.

East passes and the auction is over. North-South have won the auction in a contract of 2♠.

Suggested Opening Lead

Since North is declarer, East makes the opening lead. With a solid sequence in diamonds, East leads the ♦J, top of the solid sequence.

Declarer's Plan

After East leads, South puts the dummy hand on the table. North's goal is to take at least eight tricks to make the contract. North starts by counting the sure tricks available from the North and South hands. North counts four sure heart tricks and two diamond tricks, for a total of six. Two more are required.

North browses Declarer's Checklist. With nine spades between the combined hands, North can hope to develop at

---

DECLARER'S PLAN—THE ABC'S

Declarer: North   Contract: 2♠

ASSESS THE SITUATION

Goal	8
Sure Tricks	6
Extra Tricks Needed	2

BROWSE DECLARER'S CHECKLIST

Promotion	
Length	2 in spades
Finesse	
Trumping in dummy	

CONSIDER THE ORDER

- Draw trumps first.
- Develop the extra spade tricks early.

---

least two tricks through length provided the four missing spades are divided as expected, 3-1. If they are divided 2-2, declarer would get three tricks through length; if they are divided 4-0, declarer would still establish one trick. The club suit offers the chance to develop a trick through promotion but that won't be necessary since declarer has enough tricks from the other suits.

After winning the first diamond trick, declarer should start by leading a spade, giving up a trick to the defenders. This has the advantage of drawing the defenders' trumps so that they can not trump any of declarer's winners in the other suits. At the same time declarer is starting early to establish spade winners through length.

The defenders will be able to take three spade tricks and the ♣A and ♣K, but that's all. Declarer will finish with eight tricks.

If declarer tried to take the heart winners before drawing any trumps, the contract could be defeated. East can ruff the third round of hearts with the ♠K. West would still have the ♠A-Q-J left to take three more trump tricks. Together with the ♣A and ♣K, the defenders could now take six tricks, defeating the contract by one trick.

DEAL: 10	♠ Q J 8 3
DEALER: EAST	♥ 9
	♦ 8 7
	♣ K Q 9 7 4 2

♠ K 9 6 4
♥ K 7 5 2
♦ 9 6 5 2
♣ 5

NORTH
WEST   EAST
SOUTH

♠ A 7
♥ A Q J 6 4 3
♦ J 4 3
♣ A 10

♠ 10 5 2
♥ 10 8
♦ A K Q 10
♣ J 8 6 3

Suggested Bidding

WEST	NORTH	EAST	SOUTH
		1♥	PASS
2♥	PASS	3♥	PASS
4♥	PASS		

East has 16 high-card points plus 2 length points for the six-card suit. With a total of 18 valuation points, East opens the bidding 1♥.

South has 10 high-card points, not enough to enter the auction at this point. South passes.

West has four-card support for East's 1♥ opening bid and 6 high-card points. Since West is planning to raise partner's suit, West can value the distribution using dummy points and count 3 points for the singleton club. The total of 9 valuation points is enough to raise to the two level, showing support and about 6–10 points.

North has 8 high-card points and 2 length points for the six-card suit. North would have to bid at the three level to suggest clubs as the trump suit and chooses to pass.

With 18 points, East knows the partnership may have enough combined strength if responder has 8 or 9 points for the raise to the two level. East invites partner to bid game by rebidding 3♥.

With 9 points, West is near the top of the range and accepts the invitation by going to the game bonus level of 4♥. Everyone else passes and the auction is over. East-West are in a game contract of 4♥ and East will be the declarer.

Suggested Opening Lead

South, on declarer's left, is on lead against the 4♥ contract. South leads the ♦A, top of the solid sequence in that suit.

Declarer's Plan

After South makes the opening lead and the West hand comes down as the dummy, East makes a plan. As declarer, East's goal is to take at least ten tricks to make the 4♥ contract. East begins by counting the winners: two spades, six sure heart winners, and one club. That's a total of nine. One more trick is required.

Moving on to the second stage of the plan, East browses Declarer's Checklist. Since declarer has

```
┌─ DECLARER'S PLAN—THE ABC'S ─┐
  Declarer: East      Contract: 4♥

  ASSESS THE SITUATION
    Goal                    10
    Sure Tricks              9
    Extra Tricks Needed      1

  BROWSE DECLARER'S CHECKLIST
    Promotion
    Length
    Finesse
    Trumping in dummy   1 in clubs

  CONSIDER THE ORDER
    • Draw trumps first.
    • Keep a trump in dummy to ruff a
      club.
└──────────────────────────────┘
```

more clubs than dummy, there is a chance to gain a trick by ruffing declarer's ♣10 with one of dummy's trumps. Declarer will get seven trump tricks instead of six, enough to make the contract.

South will likely take the first three diamond tricks. If South leads a fourth round, declarer can ruff.

Declarer can start by drawing trumps. Since the three missing trumps are divided 2-1, that takes two rounds. Declarer should stop playing the trump suit at that point because declarer wants to leave at least one trump in the dummy to ruff a club.

Declarer can take a trick with the ♣A and then lead the ♣10 and ruff it with one of dummy's trumps. Now declarer can take the remaining heart and spade tricks to make the contract. The only tricks declarer loses are the first three diamond tricks.

DEAL: 11			
DEALER: SOUTH			

♠ A K 8 3
♥ A 10 8 5 3
♦ 9 6
♣ A K

	NORTH	
♠ 10 6		♠ 9
♥ K	WEST EAST	♥ Q J 9 7 2
♦ K J 7 5 2		♦ A Q 3
♣ J 10 9 8 5	SOUTH	♣ 7 6 3 2

♠ Q J 7 5 4 2
♥ 6 4
♦ 10 8 4
♣ Q 4

Suggested Bidding

WEST	NORTH	EAST	SOUTH
			PASS
PASS	1♥	PASS	1♠
PASS	4♠	PASS	PASS
PASS			

South is the dealer and has 5 high-card points plus 2 length points for the six-card suit. The total of 7 points is not enough to open.

West has 8 high-card points plus 1 point for each five-card suit for a total of 10 valuation points. With fewer than 13 points, West also passes.

North has 18 high-card points plus 1 length point for the five-card suit. North opens the bidding in the five-card major suit, 1♥.

East has 9 high-card points plus 1 length point for the five-card suit. East passes.

The auction returns to South. South doesn't have support for opener's suit. South would need at least three hearts to be sure of an eight-card fit. South does have 7 valuation points, enough to respond and to suggest a different trump suit at the one level. South responds 1♠.

West passes and the auction comes back to North who has support for partner's spade suit and can revalue the hand counting dummy points. That gives North a total of 20 points: 18 high-card points plus 1 dummy point for each doubleton. Since South has promised at least 6 points, North knows the partnership has enough combined strength for a game contract and raises all the way to 4♠.

North's 4♠ bid is followed by three passes and the auction is over.

Suggested Opening Lead

West on declarer's left makes the opening lead. With a solid three-card sequence, West can lead the ♣J, top of the touching cards.

Declarer's Plan

South's goal is to take at least ten tricks. South counts on six tricks from the spade suit, one trick in hearts, and two tricks in clubs. One more trick is needed.

South browses Declarer's Checklist for ways to develop the extra trick. Since declarer has one more diamond than dummy, the possibility exists for ruffing a diamond in the dummy. Declarer will first have to lose two diamond tricks but can then get an extra trick by trumping a diamond.

```
┌─ DECLARER'S PLAN—THE ABC'S ─┐
 Declarer: South     Contract: 4♠

 ASSESS THE SITUATION
 Goal                        10
 Sure Tricks                  9
 Extra Tricks Needed          1

 BROWSE DECLARER'S CHECKLIST
 Promotion
 Length
 Finesse
 Trumping in dummy   1 in diamonds

 CONSIDER THE ORDER
 • Draw trumps first.
 • Keep a trump in dummy to ruff a
   diamond.
```

After North wins the first club trick, South should next draw the defenders' trumps. This takes two rounds. South can then stop taking tricks in the spade suit because a trump is needed in dummy to ruff the diamond. South can lead a diamond, giving up a trick to the defenders. Declarer goes after the diamond suit early, while it is still possible to regain the lead in other suits.

Suppose the defenders lead another club. Declarer wins this trick and gives up a second diamond trick. If the defenders now lead a heart, declarer can win with dummy's ♥A and come to the South hand with a trump winner[20]. Now declarer leads the last diamond and ruffs with dummy's trump. That's declarer's tenth trick and the contract is made. Declarer loses only two diamond tricks and one heart.

---

[20] Declarer could also give up a heart trick, planning to ruff a heart to get back to the South hand.

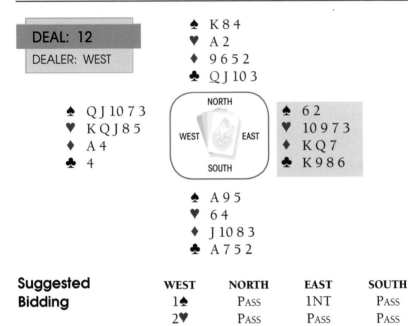

DEAL: 12

DEALER: WEST

NORTH
♠ K 8 4
♥ A 2
♦ 9 6 5 2
♣ Q J 10 3

WEST
♠ Q J 10 7 3
♥ K Q J 8 5
♦ A 4
♣ 4

EAST
♠ 6 2
♥ 10 9 7 3
♦ K Q 7
♣ K 9 8 6

SOUTH
♠ A 9 5
♥ 6 4
♦ J 10 8 3
♣ A 7 5 2

Suggested	**WEST**	**NORTH**	**EAST**	**SOUTH**
Bidding	1♠	PASS	1NT	PASS
	2♥	PASS	PASS	PASS

West is the dealer and values the hand. There are 15 valuation points: 13 high-card points plus 1 length point for each five-card suit. That's more than enough to open the bidding. With a choice between two five-card major suits, West follows the guideline to open the higher-ranking, 1♠.

North has the next opportunity to bid. With only 10 high-card points, North passes.

East is the responder to the 1♠ opening. With 8 high-card points, East has enough to respond. East wants to keep the auction going in case West has a strong hand of about 18 or more points and there is enough combined strength for game. With only two spades, East doesn't have enough to raise. There is no room left on the Bidding Ladder to suggest a different trump suit at the one level and East doesn't have enough strength to suggest a new suit at the two level. Instead, East bids 1NT, the only option remaining.

South passes and the auction returns to West. Since East didn't show support for spades, West can now suggest another suit as trumps by bidding 2♥. North passes.

East prefers hearts to spades as the trump suit. Since West hasn't shown any extra strength, East can pass and leave the partnership in its best partscore. South also passes and the auction is over.

Suggested Opening Lead

North, to declarer's left, makes the opening lead. With a solid sequence in clubs, North leads the ♣Q, the top of the touching cards.

Declarer's Plan

As declarer, West needs to take eight tricks to make the 2♥ contract. The only immediate winners are in the diamond suit, the ♦A, ♦K, and ♦Q. West will need to establish five more tricks to make the contract.

Browsing Declarer's Checklist, West can plan to promote four winners in the heart suit by driving out the defenders' ♥A. In addition, at least one winner can be promoted in the spade suit by driving out the

> ### DECLARER'S PLAN—THE ABC'S
>
> Declarer: West   Contract: 2♥
>
> **ASSESS THE SITUATION**
>
> | | |
> |---|---|
> | Goal | 8 |
> | Sure Tricks | 3 |
> | Extra Tricks Needed | 5 |
>
> **BROWSE DECLARER'S CHECKLIST**
>
> | | |
> |---|---|
> | Promotion | 4 in hearts |
> | 1 in spades | |
> | Length | |
> | Finesse | |
> | Trumping in dummy | |
>
> **CONSIDER THE ORDER**
>
> - Draw trumps and promote hearts.
> - Develop the extra spade trick early.

defender's ♠A and ♠K. That's all the tricks that are needed, although declarer might see the additional possibility of developing a spade trick through length or by ruffing a spade in the dummy.

The defenders will win the first trick whether or not declarer chooses to play dummy's ♣K. If the defenders try to take a second trick in the suit, declarer can ruff. Declarer now goes to work on the heart suit. This has the two-fold advantage of drawing the defenders' trumps and promoting the winners in the heart suit.

After losing a trick to the defenders' ♥A, declarer will eventually regain the lead and can finish drawing the trumps. Then declarer can go to work promoting a winner in the spade suit. The only tricks declarer will likely lose are the ♠A, ♠K, ♥A, and a club trick.

Bridge provides the kind of mental acuity that is handy for anything you want to do with excellence.

—Bill Gates

Minor Suit Opening Bids and Responses

The 1♣ and 1♦ Opening Bids

If you have enough strength to open the bidding but the hand doesn't meet the requirements for 1NT or an opening bid in a major suit, the only option left is an opening bid in a minor suit. An opening bid of 1♣ or 1♦ requires two features:

OPENING 1♣ OR 1♦

- 13–21 valuation points.
- A three-card or longer suit.

With a choice between 1♣ and 1♦:

- The longer minor suit is opened.
- With equal length in both minors:
  - Open 1♦ with four or more cards.
  - Open 1♣ with two three-card suits.

The Strength

The range for an opening bid of 1♣ or 1♦ is the same as 1♥ or 1♠. It starts with the minimum requirement of 13 valuation points and goes up to very strong hands of about 21 points. As mentioned earlier, hands with 22 or more points are opened at the two level but are rare and left for a later book (POPULAR CONVENTIONS).

The Length

It might seem strange that an opening bid of 1♣ or 1♦ can be made on as few as three cards but it's because of the five-card major approach. A hand with one or two four-card major suits can't be opened 1♥ or 1♠. As a result, an opening bid of 1♣ or 1♦ will occasionally be made with a three-card suit. This is the exception, however. 1♣ and 1♦ are usually opened with a four-card or longer suit.

Examples

The following hands have the requirements to open in a minor:

♠ K 8 4 ♥ A 9 ♦ Q J 7 5 ♣ K 8 3 2	Open 1♦. The hand is balanced but there are only 13 high-card points, not enough for 1NT. With a choice of four-card minor suits, open the higher-ranking, diamonds.
♠ A Q 9 4 ♥ 8 ♦ A K 3 ♣ A J 8 7 5	Open 1♣. This hand has 18 high-card points plus 1 length point for the five-card suit. With an unbalanced hand and no five-card major suit, open the longer minor suit.
♠ K 9 7 5 ♥ A Q 7 3 ♦ A 8 3 ♣ J 4	Open 1♦. You have to open a three-card minor suit with this type of hand. There are only 14 high-card points, too few to open 1NT. You can't open either major suit because that would promise a five-card suit. With nothing else to do, open the longer minor suit.

♠ A K J 6	Open 1♣. A balanced hand with 19 high-card
♥ K Q 4	points, too strong for 1NT. With no five-card
♦ K 7 2	major, open a minor. With a choice between two
♣ K 9 3	three-card suits, the standard opening is 1♣.

The following hands do not have the requirements to open in a minor suit:

♠ A Q 3	1NT. There are 15 high-card points plus 1
♥ Q 7	length point for the five-card suit. With a bal-
♦ K Q 10 9 6	anced hand that falls in the 15–17 point range,
♣ Q 9 8	open 1NT.

♠ 8	Open 1♥. There are 13 high-card points plus 1
♥ Q 10 7 5 3	length point for each five-card suit. With two
♦ A K J 10 6	five-card suits, open the higher-ranking, hearts.
♣ K 4	The quality of the two suits doesn't matter.

Responding to an Opening Bid of 1♣ or 1♦

Minor suit opening bids have some similarities to major suit opening bids. They are much less specific about opener's strength and distribution than a 1NT opening bid which shows 15–17 points and a balanced hand. Opener could have from 13 to 21 points and might have a balanced hand or a very unbalanced hand. Responder can't immediately determine How High and Where to place the contract. As a result, responder can't sign off except by passing.

Responder's bids are invitational or forcing. The general approach, therefore, is similar to responding to a major suit. Responder can get more information by making a forcing bid in a new suit, or can make a limited, invitational bid by raising opener's suit or bidding notrump.

There's one big difference, however. Responder's priority after an opening bid of 1♥ or 1♠ is to consider supporting opener's suit. Responder's priority after an opening bid of 1♣ or 1♦ is to look for a major suit fit.

Responder's Priority – Finding a Major Suit Fit

The way the game bonus levels are structured, the partnership priority is to look for an eight-card or longer major suit fit. Game in hearts or spades requires ten tricks; game in clubs or diamonds requires eleven. If there is a fit in both a major suit and a minor suit, the major suit is preferred. Even in partscore, major suit contracts score higher than the equivalent minor suit contracts (see Appendix 2). Since a new suit is forcing, responder needs values to bid. With 0–5 points, responder should pass before getting the partnership any higher.

With 6 or more points, in response to an opening bid of 1♣ or 1♦, responder's first priority is to bid a major suit:

RESPONDING 1♥ OR 1♠
6 or more valuation points.
A four-card or longer suit.

An opening bid of 1♥ or 1♠ promises a five-card or longer suit, but a response of 1♥ or 1♠ can be made on as few as four cards in the suit. Opener will often have a four-card major suit, and if neither partner could bid a four-card suit, the partnership would never find its eight-card fit.

Choice of Suits

With a choice of suits to bid at the one level, responder bids the longest. With a choice among suits of equal length, use the following guideline:

RESPONDER'S CHOICE OF SUITS

- With a choice of four-card suits, bid the cheapest—the one that comes next on the Bidding Ladder.
- With a choice of five-card suits, bid the higher-ranking.

Bidding the cheapest four-card suit is referred to as bidding *up the line*.

Examples of Responding in a New Suit at the One Level—Forcing

Here are examples of responding to an opening bid in a minor suit.

| Your partner opens 1♣ | ◄——— | 13–21 points; three-card or longer suit |

♠ 8 2
♥ J 7 6 3
♦ Q 9 8 6 4
♣ 9 3

Pass. You don't like clubs as a trump suit, but with only 3 high-card points plus 1 length point, you don't have enough to respond. The 1♣ opening isn't forcing. Partner could have only three clubs but is more likely to have four, five or six. If you bid, the partnership is likely to get much too high because a response in a new suit is forcing.

♠ A J 8 4
♥ 9 2
♦ 8 6
♣ K J 10 5 3

1♠. You have support for partner's clubs but the priority is to look for a major suit fit. If you can't find a fit in spades, you can always show the club support later. You only need a four-card suit when responding in a major at the one level.

♠ A Q 8 3
♥ K J 9 6 5
♦ Q 7
♣ 5 4

1♥. You have 13 valuation points: 12 high-card points plus 1 length point. The combined partnership strength is enough to go to a bonus level but the first step is to find a trump fit. With a choice of suits, bid the longer.

♠ Q 9 7 5 3
♥ 8 4
♦ K Q 8 6 5
♣ 7

1♠. There are 7 high-card points plus 1 length point for each five-card suit. With two five-card suits, bid the higher-ranking.

| Your partner opens 1♣ | ◄── | 13–21 points; three-card or longer suit |

♠ K J 7 5
♥ Q J 6 2
♦ 8 3
♣ A 7 5

1♥. With a choice of four-card suits, bid up the line, cheaper first. With a fit for hearts, partner can raise. With no heart fit, opener can bid 1♠ with a four-card suit and a spade fit will be found. If there's no fit in either major, the partnership will play in notrump or clubs.

♠ K Q 8 3
♥ 7 5 4
♦ Q 9 7 4
♣ 10 2

1♠ (1♦). Although four-card suits are usually bid up the line, an exception can be made when one of the suits is diamonds. Because of the priority on finding a major suit fit, most players would respond 1♠ with this hand.

Responder's Second Choice—Notrump—Invitational

The partnership will usually consider a notrump contract ahead of a minor suit contract. Game in notrump requires nine tricks. Game in clubs or diamonds requires eleven tricks. Notrump partscores are also worth more than the equivalent minor suit partscore.

With a balanced hand but no four-card major suit to bid, responder can use the following guideline:

RESPONDING IN NOTRUMP TO 1♣ OR 1♦	
6–10 points	Respond 1NT
11–12 points	Respond 2NT
13–15 points	Respond 3NT

A response in notrump is non-forcing[21]. Opener can pass if satisfied that the partnership is in the best contract.

---

[21] Some partnerships prefer a 2NT response to show 13–15 points and a 3NT response to show 16–18 points. In that style, the 2NT response is forcing because the partnership has enough combined strength for game. The recommended style has become more popular.

Examples of Responding in Notrump—Invitational

Your partner opens 1♦ ← 13–21 points; three-card or longer suit

♠ Q 9 4
♥ K 7 3
♦ J 8 3
♣ Q 6 5 3

1NT. There are 8 high-card points. You don't have a four-card major suit, don't have enough strength to bid a new suit at the two level, and can't support diamonds with only three cards in the suit. You're showing about 6-10 points with the 1NT response.

♠ K J 5
♥ Q J 7
♦ 9 7 4 2
♣ A J 5

2NT. Although you have support for diamonds, suggest notrump with such a balanced hand. Jumping to 2NT shows about 11–12 points and is highly invitational. With a bare minimum opening, however, partner can pass and the partnership will stop in partscore.

♠ A J 7
♥ K 10 9
♦ Q J 4
♣ K 9 7 2

3NT. With 14 high-card points opposite opener's 13 or more points, the partnership has enough combined strength for a game contract. Suggest playing game in notrump. Partner will usually pass.

♠ Q 10 8 5
♥ K 7 5
♦ 10 4
♣ A 10 8 3

1♠. The hand is balanced, but the priority is to look for a major suit fit. If you were to respond 1NT you would be denying a four-card or longer major suit.

Responder's Third Choice—Raising Opener's Minor Suit— Invitational

Minor suit contracts are not a priority for the partnership, but there are times when there's no major suit fit and the hand is unsuitable for a notrump contract. As the final option, responder can suggest the partnership play in a minor suit.

```
RAISING OPENER'S MINOR SUIT
6–10 POINTS     RAISE TO THE TWO LEVEL.
11–12 POINTS    RAISE TO THE THREE LEVEL.
13+ POINTS      GET TO THE GAME LEVEL.
```

When responder has 13 or more points, there is enough combined strength to go for a game bonus. Jumping directly to 5♣ or 5♦, however, is not a good idea unless responder has a very unbalanced hand. Minor suit game contracts require about 28 or 29 points. Since game in notrump can often be made with as few as 25 or 26 points, the partnership usually wants to explore this possibility first.

Trump Support for Opener's Minor Suit

There's a difference between raising a major suit and a minor suit. An opening bid of 1♥ or 1♠ shows a five-card or longer suit but an opening bid of 1♣ or 1♦ could be made on as few as three cards. To guarantee an eight-card fit, responder would need five-card or longer support for the minor suit. In practice, however, opener will usually have a four-card or longer minor suit. A four-card, five-card, and six-card minor suit are all more likely than a three-card suit. So:

Responder can consider raising a minor with four-card or longer support.

As seen previously, however, there are usually other options.

Valuing Dummy Points When Supporting a Minor Suit

With support for partner's minor suit and shortness in another suit, revalue the hand counting dummy points in place of length points. There is, however, a caution. A short suit is likely to be valuable if the partnership does play with the minor suit as trumps. If the partnership is headed toward the game level, the emphasis is on playing in notrump rather than a minor suit. In a notrump contract, shortness will be a liability rather than an asset. As a guideline, avoid counting dummy points when raising opener's minor suit unless your hand is very unbalanced and you have no intention of playing in notrump.

Examples of Raising Opener's Minor Suit—Invitational

| Your partner opens 1♦ | ← | 13–21 points; three-card or longer suit |

♠ 8 4
♥ 6 3
♦ K J 7 5 3
♣ Q J 6 2

2♦. You don't have a four-card suit that can be bid at the one level. With 9 valuation points, there is enough to respond, and you have support for opener's suit. Raise to the two level.

♠ 9 8 3
♥ 7
♦ A Q 9 8 5 2
♣ K 10 3

3♦. There are 9 high-card points plus 2 length points for the six-card suit. That's too much to raise to 2♦ but not enough to commit to game. Make an invitational raise to the three level. If you counted 3 dummy points for the singleton heart instead of the 2 length points, you would still make the same response. If opener chooses to bid 3NT, however, the singleton heart won't be an asset.

♠ K 9 4
♥ Q J 7
♦ A J 9 4
♣ K 8 3

3NT. There are 14 high-card points, enough to go for a game bonus. Although you have four-card support for diamonds, the nine-trick contract of 3NT is likely to be a better choice than the eleven-trick contract of 5♦.

| Your partner opens 1♦ | ◄─── | 13–21 points; three-card or longer suit |

♠ —
♥ 3 2
♦ K J 8 7 6 5
♣ A Q 8 4 2

5♦. The hand is too unbalanced to consider a notrump contract. Since you definitely want to play in the minor suit, count 5 dummy points for the spade void and 1 for the doubleton heart in addition to the 10 high-card points. That's enough for game in the minor suit.

♠ 9 6 4
♥ 4
♦ A K 6
♣ K Q 10 8 7 4

2♣. You have an unbalanced hand but don't want to raise diamonds right away with only three-card support. Instead, show your own minor suit. You have enough strength to bid a new suit at the two level. The 2♣ response is forcing and you can decide what to do next after hearing opener's rebid.

Opener's Rebid

If responder has bid a new suit, opener can't pass. Opener chooses a rebid that best describes both the strength and distribution of the hand, leaving the next decision to responder.

If responder has made a bid that limits the strength of responder's hand to a narrow range, opener can pass if the partnership appears to be in the best contract. For example, if responder bids 1NT, showing 6–10 points, opener could pass with a minimum-strength balanced hand, knowing the partnership has found its best contract and that there isn't enough combined strength to go for the game bonus.

Opener's Rebid After Responder Bids a New Suit

After opener bids 1♣ or 1♦ and responder bids a new suit, opener has a lot of choices which include:

- Raising responder's suit with support.
- Bidding a new suit at the one level.

- Bidding a new suit at the two level.
- Bidding notrump to show a balanced hand.
- Rebidding the original suit.

Opener Raises Responder's Suit

With support for responder's suit[22], opener revalues the hand using dummy points—5 for a void, 3 for a singleton, 1 for a doubleton—and describes the strength of the hand by raising to the appropriate level using the following guideline:

OPENER'S REBID — RAISING RESPONDER'S SUIT		
Minimum Hand	13–16 points	Raise to the two level.
Medium Hand	17–18 points	Raise to the three level.
Maximum Hand	19–21 points	Raise to the game level.

Here are examples after responder bids a new suit at the one level and opener has support for the suit.

OPENER (YOU)	RESPONDER (PARTNER)
13–21 points; a three-card or longer suit ▶ 1♦ ?	1♠ ◀ 6+ points; 4+ spades

♠ J 7 5 3
♥ A 8 3
♦ K Q 8 7
♣ K 10

2♠. Responder has shown a four-card or longer spade suit so the partnership has at least an eight-card trump fit. This hand has 13 high-card points and you can revalue to include 1 dummy point for the doubleton club. The hand is still in the minimum-strength opening bid category, so raise as cheaply as possible.

---

[22] Ideally, opener should have four-card support, since responder may have a four-card suit. In practice, opener often raises with three-card support and an unbalanced hand.

♠ A 10 8 3
♥ 4
♦ A Q 7 5 4 2
♣ K 8

3♦. The hand has 13 high-card points plus 3 dummy points for the singleton heart and 1 dummy point for the doubleton club. The total of 17 valuation points is enough to put this in the medium-strength category as an opening bid. Show the extra strength with a jump raise to the three level. This is still invitational. Responder can pass with only 6 or 7 points.

♠ K Q 8 5
♥ 3 2
♦ A K J 6
♣ A Q 5

4♠. 19 high-card points plus 1 dummy point puts this hand in the maximum-strength category. Having found a major suit fit, take the partnership all the way to the game bonus level. Even if responder has as few as 6 points, the partnership has enough combined strength for game.

Opener Bids a New Suit at the One Level

If opener doesn't have a fit for responder's suit, opener can continue the search for a suitable suit by bidding a second suit at the one level. For example:

OPENER (YOU)	RESPONDER (PARTNER)
13–21 points; a three-card or longer suit ► 1♣ ?	1♥ ◄ 6+ points; 4+ hearts

♠ K J 7 4
♥ 9 4
♦ K J 3
♣ A J 8 7

1♠. Opener doesn't have a fit for responder's hearts but can conveniently continue the search by showing the four-card spade suit at the one level. Responder could have four spades as well as four or more hearts. Responder won't expect opener to have a five-card suit for the rebid, since opener could start with 1♠ with a five-card suit.

Opener Shows a Balanced Hand

If opener can't support responder's suit and doesn't have a second suit that can be bid at the one level, the next priority is to show a balanced hand. A balanced hand with 15-17 points would have been opened 1NT, so opener has either a weaker balanced hand or a stronger balanced hand. With a balanced hand of fewer than 15 points, opener rebids 1NT; with a balanced hand of 18 or more points, opener jumps to 2NT. For example:

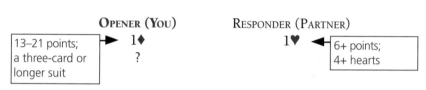

OPENER (YOU)   RESPONDER (PARTNER)

13–21 points; a three-card or longer suit   1♦   1♥   6+ points; 4+ hearts

?

♠ K 9 5
♥ Q 7
♦ A J 8 5 2
♣ Q 10 5

1NT. You have a balanced hand worth 13 valuation points: 12 high-card points plus 1 length point for the five-card suit. With no fit for hearts and no second suit that can be bid at the one level, opener describes a minimum-strength balanced hand by bidding notrump at the cheapest level.

♠ A Q J
♥ J 4
♦ A Q 8 4
♣ K Q 7 3

2NT. This balanced hand has 19 high-card points. You start with 1♦ and jump in notrump to show a balanced hand too strong to open 1NT. Showing the balanced hand takes priority over showing a second suit at the two level.

Opener Bids a New Suit at the Two Level

With an unbalanced hand, opener can bid a second suit at the two level. For example:

OPENER (YOU)

13–21 points; a three-card or longer suit ► 1♦
?

RESPONDER (PARTNER)

1♠ ◄ 6+ points; 4+ spades

♠ 5
♥ K 6 3
♦ A K 7 5 2
♣ A J 8 4

2♣. Opener can't support responder's major suit, can't bid a new suit at the one level, and doesn't have a balanced hand. Having already shown the diamond suit, opener can now show the club suit and leave the next decision to responder.

Opener Rebids the Original Suit

If opener's hand is unbalanced but opener doesn't have a second suit to bid, the last option is to rebid the original suit. For example:

OPENER (YOU)

13–21 points; a three-card or longer suit ► 1♣
?

RESPONDER (PARTNER)

1♥ ◄ 6+ points; 4+ hearts

♠ 7 4 3
♥ 4
♦ A 8 5
♣ A K J 8 7 5

2♣. Opener doesn't have support for responder's suit, doesn't have a second suit to show, and doesn't have a balanced hand. Opener simply rebids the original suit, showing the extra length there. With a minimum-strength opening bid, opener rebids the suit at the cheapest level.

♠ 4
♥ A 5
♦ K 8 2
♣ A Q J 10 8 7 4

3♣. This hand has 14 high-card points plus 3 length points for the seven-card suit. That puts it in the medium-strength category. To show the extra strength, opener can rebid the suit jumping a level. This is highly invitational, but responder can still pass and settle for partscore with a minimum response.

Opener's Rebid After a Notrump Response

If responder bids notrump, opener isn't forced to bid again because responder has limited the strength of the hand. With a balanced hand, opener can pass, invite game, or bid game depending on the combined strength. With an unbalanced hand, opener can show a second suit or rebid the original suit. Here are some examples after responder has bid 1NT, showing 6–10 points.

	OPENER (YOU)	RESPONDER (PARTNER)	
13–21 points; a three-card or longer suit	1♦ ?	1NT	6–10 points; invitational

♠ Q 8 2
♥ K J 4
♦ A 10 8 4
♣ K 9 3

Pass. Opener has 13 high-card points so the combined partnership strength is from 19–23 points, not enough to try for a game bonus. With a balanced hand, opener passes and leaves the partnership in a notrump partscore.

♠ A K 8 3
♥ 3 2
♦ K Q 7 5
♣ J 10 4

Pass. Although opener has a four-card major suit, it isn't worth showing it because there won't be an eight-card fit. Responder's priority was to show a four-card or longer major suit at the one level. Having bypassed spades, responder can't have four cards in the suit. With a balanced hand and a minimum opening bid, opener settles for partscore in notrump.

♠ K 4
♥ 5
♦ A J 8 7 3
♣ K Q 9 6 5

2♣. With an unbalanced hand opener doesn't want to play in notrump. Instead, opener shows the second suit, suggesting responder choose between diamonds and clubs as the trump suit.

♠ Q 8 4
♥ Q 4
♦ A K J 8 7
♣ A J 5

2NT. Opener has 18 valuation points: 17 high-card points plus 1 length point for the five-card diamond suit. The partnership has somewhere between 24 and 28 points. Opener invites responder to bid game with the top of the range for the 1NT response. Responder can pass with the bottom of the range.

Here are some examples after responder has bid 2NT, showing 11–12 points.

OPENER (YOU)		RESPONDER (PARTNER)	
13–21 points; a three-card or longer suit	1♣ ?	2NT	11–12 points; balanced, invitational

♠ A 6
♥ Q J 8 4
♦ Q 8 2
♣ K J 7 3

Pass. With a bare minimum of 13 high-card points for the opening bid, opener rejects responder's invitation. There's no point in bidding hearts; with a four-card or longer heart suit, responder would have bid 1♥ rather than 2NT.

♠ 6 4
♥ A J 5
♦ Q 5
♣ A Q J 8 7 5

3NT. With 14 high-card points plus 2 length points, opener has enough to take the partnership to game. Although the hand is slightly unbalanced, it should be easier to take nine tricks in notrump than eleven tricks in a contract of 5♣.

Opener's Rebid After Responder Raises Opener's Minor

If responder raises opener's minor suit, opener isn't forced to bid again because responder has limited the strength of the hand by the level of the raise. Opener can pass, invite game, or bid game depending on the combined strength.

Here are examples after responder raises a 1♦ opening to the two level, showing support and 6–10 points.

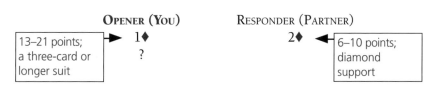

OPENER (YOU)	RESPONDER (PARTNER)
13–21 points; a three-card or longer suit → 1♦	2♦ ← 6–10 points; diamond support
?	

♠ A J 7 2
♥ K 9 6 2
♦ K Q 4
♣ 7 2

Pass. You have only 13 high-card points and responder has at most 10 so the partnership belongs in partscore. There's no point bidding hearts or spades because responder would have bid 1♥ or 1♠ with a four-card suit. Responder is likely to have five-card support, so don't be concerned about the three-card suit.

♠ 7
♥ 6 4 2
♦ A K J 7 5 3 2
♣ A Q

3♦. There are 14 high-card points plus 3 length points for the seven-card suit. The hand is in the medium-strength category for an opening bid. Raising to 3♦ invites responder to bid again with the top of the range for the raise. Otherwise, the partnership will stop in partscore.

♠ K J
♥ A Q J 7
♦ K 10 8 6 3
♣ K Q

3NT. There are 19 high-card points plus 1 length point for the fifth diamond. The partnership has at least 26 combined points, enough to go for the game bonus. 3NT should be an easier contract than 5♦. There's no need to mention the heart suit. With four or more hearts, responder would have bid 1♥ rather than raise to 2♦.

Responder's Rebid

By the time it comes to responder's rebid, responder should have a good description of opener's strength and distribution. Responder should be able to decide **How High** and **Where**. For example:

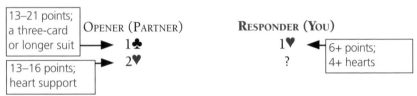

13–21 points; a three-card or longer suit	Opener (Partner)		Responder (You)	
	▶ 1♣		1♥	6+ points; 4+ hearts
13–16 points; heart support	▶ 2♥		?	

♠ K 9 7 5
♥ Q 10 7 4
♦ Q 6 2
♣ 8 4

Pass. Opener's raise to the cheapest level shows a minimum-strength opening bid. You have only 7 high-card points so you know **How High**. There isn't enough combined strength for a game contract. The partnership has found a suitable trump fit, so you know **Where**. Pass, and play in partscore.

♠ 7 6 3
♥ A 10 8 7 5
♦ K 4
♣ K 8 5

3♥. Your hand is worth 10 high-card points plus 1 length point for the five-card suit. Partner has shown a minimum-strength opening of about 13 to 16 points. A game bonus is possible if opener is at the top of the range. To settle **How High**, invite by raising to the three level. The partnership can stop in partscore if opener has nothing extra. You have found a heart fit, so you know **Where**.

♠ 5 4
♥ A J 9 7 6 3
♦ A 9 4
♣ Q 7

4♥. You have 11 high-card points plus 2 length points. Even if opener has only 13 points, the partnership has enough to try for the game bonus. That tells you **How High**. You've found a major suit fit, so you also have the answer to **Where**. Jump to game in hearts and see if you can make ten tricks.

Declarer's Plan – The ABC's

Assess the Situation

- Goal
- Sure Tricks
- Extra Tricks Needed

When there are enough sure tricks, declarer goes ahead and takes them. If there are not enough sure tricks, declarer moves to the second step of the plan.

Browse Declarer's Checklist to Develop Extra Tricks

Promotion and length are useful ways to develop extra tricks in both notrump and suit contracts. Another technique that can be used in both notrump and suit contracts is the *finesse*.

- Promotion
- Length
- The Finesse
- Trumping in dummy

DUMMY
♥ K 5

DECLARER
♥ 7 2

The finesse is a method for developing tricks when the opponents have one or more higher cards. The principle of the finesse is to lead toward the card you hope will take a trick. Here is an example where you are missing the ♥A but would like to take a trick with the ♥K.

Since the defenders hold the ♥A, it won't do any good to lead the ♥K. It also won't help to lead a low heart from the dummy since the defenders can win with one of their other high cards and retain the ♥A to capture the ♥K.

Instead, take a finesse by leading a low heart from declarer's hand toward the card you hope will take a trick, the ♥K. You are hoping the full layout of the suit is something like this:

DUMMY
♥ K 5

WEST   EAST
♥ A J 8 6   ♥ Q 10 9 4 3

DECLARER
♥ 7 2

If the West plays the ♥A, you will play the ♥5 from dummy and the ♥K will be a winner once you regain the lead. If West plays a low heart on the first trick, you will immediately play dummy's ♥K and win the trick.

The finesse succeeds only if the ♥A is favorably placed. Suppose this is the actual layout:

DUMMY
♥ K 5

WEST   EAST
♥ Q 10 9 4 3   ♥ A J 8 6

DECLARER
♥ 7 2

When declarer leads a low heart and plays dummy's ♥K, the finesse loses to the defenders' ♥A. Declarer doesn't get a trick.

Here is a situation in which declarer wants to get a trick with the ♦Q when the defenders hold the ♦K:

DUMMY
♦ A Q

DECLARER
♦ 5 4

Declarer leads a low diamond toward dummy and finesses the ♦Q. If the ♦K is favorably placed on declarer's left, the finesse succeeds and declarer has two tricks instead of one. If the ♦K is unfavorably placed on declarer's right, the finesse loses and declarer is back to the one sure trick.

Consider the Order

When it comes to the third stage of the plan, consider the order in which to play the cards, keep the following points in mind when planning to take a finesse:

1) Be in the right place at the right time. To take a finesse, lead toward the card you hope will take a trick. Plan the play so that you can lead from the appropriate hand when you are ready to take the finesse. In the previous examples a low card had to be led from declarer's hand.

2) Develop the extra tricks early. If you might lose a trick when taking a finesse, you want to do so while you still have winners in the other suits so that you can regain the lead.

Defense – Look at Dummy

Before the opening lead, the defenders can see only 13 cards. Once dummy comes down, the defenders can see an additional 13 cards, the dummy hand. They will also see the cards played to the first trick by partner and declarer. By the time the first trick is played, the defenders will have seen more than half the cards in the deck.

The defenders use this information, plus any information from the auction or partner's signals (see page 54) to form a plan for defeating the contract. Although it takes a lot of practice to watch and remember which cards have been played, here are some useful guidelines:

1) When defending against a suit contract, avoid leading a suit in which dummy is void if there is still a trump left in dummy. Declarer will be able to ruff with dummy's trump and win the trick.

2) It is often a good idea to lead through strength and up to weakness.

For example, suppose this is the layout of the heart suit around the table:

DUMMY
♥ A Q 10

WEST   EAST
♥ 8 6 2   ♥ K J 9 3

DECLARER
♥ 7 5 4

It is better for the defense if West leads this suit, through the strength in the dummy and up to the hoped for weakness in declarer's hand. If West can lead the suit twice, East will get tricks with the ♥K and ♥J. It is not good if East has to lead the suit into the strength in dummy. Then the defenders won't get a trick.

SUMMARY

Requirements for Opening 1♣ or 1♦

- 13-21 valuation points.
- A three-card or longer suit.

Responder's Priorities After 1♣ or 1♦

- Bid a major suit.
- Bid notrump.
- Support partner's minor suit.

Requirements to Respond 1♥ or 1♠

- 6 or more valuation points.
- A four-card or longer suit.
- With a choice of four-card suits, bid the cheapest—the one that comes next on the Bidding Ladder
- With a choice of five-card suits, bid the higher-ranking.

Requirements to Respond in Notrump

- 6–10 points   Respond 1NT.
- 11–12 points   Respond 2NT.
- 13–15 points   Respond 3NT.

Requirement to Raise Opener's Minor

With four-card or longer support responder can consider raising opener's minor using the following guidelines:

- 6–10 points   Raise to the two level.
- 11–12 points   Raise to the three level.
- 13–15 points   Get to the game level.

Opener's Rebid

IF RESPONDER BIDS A NEW SUIT

- With support, raise to the appropriate level.
- Bid a new suit at the one level.
- Bid a new suit at the two level.
- Bid notrump at the appropriate level.
- Rebid the original suit at the appropriate level.

IF RESPONDER BIDS NOTRUMP

Use the specific information and, based on this, decide **How High** and **Where** to place the contract.

IF RESPONDER RAISES OPENER'S MINOR SUIT

Use the specific information and, based on this, decide **How High** and **Where** to place the contract.

RESPONDER'S REBID

By the time responder rebids, opener has bid twice to describe the hand. By this time responder usually has enough information to decide **How High** and **Where** to place the contract.

		BONUS LEVEL
		(COMBINED VALUATION PTS.)
	7NT	↓
7-Level	7♠	**GRAND SLAM**
(13 Tricks)	7♥	**37+**
	7♦	
	7♣	
	6NT	
6-Level	6♠	**SMALL SLAM**
(12 Tricks)	6♥	**33+**
	6♦	
	6♣	
	5NT	
5-Level	5♠	
(11 Tricks)	5♥	
	5♦	**GAME 29+ PTS.**
	5♣	
	4NT	
4-Level	4♠	**GAME 26+ PTS.**
(10 Tricks)	4♥	
	4♦	
	4♣	
	3NT	**GAME 25+ PTS.**
3-Level	3♠	
(9 Tricks)	3♥	
	3♦	
	3♣	↑
	2NT	
2-Level	2♠	
(8 Tricks)	2♥	
	2♦	
	2♣	
	1NT	
1-Level	1♠	
(7 Tricks)	1♥	
	1♦	
	1♣	

BIDDING LADDER

Declarer's Plan—The ABCs

Assess the Situation
- Goal
- Sure Tricks
- Extra Tricks Needed

Browse Declarer's Checklist if Extra Tricks are Required
- Promotion
- Length
- The Finesse
- Trumping in dummy.

Consider the Order
- Be in the right place at the right time.
- Develop the extra tricks early.

Defense—Look at Dummy

Like declarer, the defenders should formulate a plan for defeating the contract. To do this, they have to watch the cards played and look at the dummy to help decide where their tricks are coming from and which suit to lead.

Quiz – Part I

You are the dealer. What call would you make with the following hands?

a) ♠ A K 7 4
   ♥ 3
   ♦ K J 8 4
   ♣ A J 7 5

b) ♠ K 8 7 3
   ♥ A J 10 5
   ♦ K 8 4
   ♣ Q 6

c) ♠ A Q J 3
   ♥ K J 2
   ♦ K J 7
   ♣ A 8 4

Partner opens the bidding 1♣.

OPENER (PARTNER)	RESPONDER (YOU)
1♣	?

13–21 points; a three-card or longer suit

What would you respond with each of the following hands?

d) ♠ 9 3
   ♥ J 7 5 4 2
   ♦ J 8 4
   ♣ 7 5 3

e) ♠ 6 4
   ♥ A 9 7 3
   ♦ 7 2
   ♣ K J 8 7 4

f) ♠ J 9 8 6 3
   ♥ 7
   ♦ A J 9 8 5
   ♣ 7 5

g) ♠ K Q 7 4
   ♥ Q J 8 5
   ♦ A 8 3
   ♣ 6 2

h) ♠ K 10 4
   ♥ Q J 6
   ♦ Q 10 8
   ♣ 9 7 4 3

i) ♠ K Q 9
   ♥ Q 10 8
   ♦ A J 5
   ♣ 10 8 7 5

j) ♠ A Q 8
   ♥ K 10 9
   ♦ K J 7
   ♣ Q 8 7 3

k) ♠ K 7 4
   ♥ 5
   ♦ 9 8 6 3
   ♣ Q J 9 7 5

l) ♠ 7 3
   ♥ 9 6
   ♦ K 7 5
   ♣ A Q 10 7 4 2

m) ♠ Q 9 3
   ♥ 7
   ♦ A J 8 7 6 3
   ♣ 10 8 4

n) ♠ A Q J 4
   ♥ Q 10 8 7 3
   ♦ 7 4
   ♣ 9 5

o) ♠ A K J 9 6 3
   ♥ K Q 9 4
   ♦ A 4
   ♣ 2

Answers to Quiz — Part I

a) **1♦**. The hand is unbalanced and there is no five-card major suit. With a choice of four-card minor suits, open 1♦. (HIGHER RANK)

b) **1♦**. The hand is balanced but there are only 13 high-card points. With no five-card major, open the longer minor.

c) **1♣**. There are 19 high-card points, too many to open 1NT. With no five-card major, open in a minor suit. With a choice between two three-card minors, open 1♣. (LOWER RANK)

d) **Pass**. With fewer than 6 points, pass and stop in partscore.

e) **1♥**. There are 8 high-card points plus 1 length point, enough to respond. Although you have support for clubs, the priority is to look for a major suit fit.

f) **1♠**. There are 6 high-card points plus 1 length point for each five-card suit. With a choice between two five-card suits, bid the higher-ranking.

g) **1♥**. There are 12 high-card points. With a choice of four-card suits to bid at the one level, bid the lower-ranking.

h) **1NT**. With 8 high-card points and a balanced hand, respond 1NT, showing 6–10 points and no four-card or longer major.

i) **2NT**. This hand has 12 high-card points. With no four-card major suit to bid and a balanced hand, jump to 2NT.

j) **3NT**. There are 15 high-card points. With no four-card major, showing a balanced hand takes priority over showing support for the minor suit. The partnership has enough for game.

k) **2♣**. With an unbalanced hand and five-card support, raise opener's minor with no four-card or longer major suit. A raise to the two level shows 6–10 points.

l) **3♣**. With 9 high-card points plus 2 length points, this hand is worth an invitational jump raise to the three level, showing 11–12 points.

m) **1♦**. A new suit at the one level shows 6 or more points and is forcing.

n) **1♥**. With a choice of suits at the one level, bid the longer suit.

o) **1♠**. A new suit response at the one level is unlimited in the upper range of strength.

Quiz – Part II

You open the bidding 1♦ and partner responds 1♥.

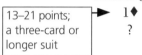
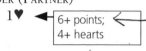

OPENER (YOU)	**RESPONDER (PARTNER)**
1♦	1♥

13–21 points;
a three-card or
longer suit

?   6+ points;
4+ hearts

*(or many
more)*

What do you rebid with each of the following hands?

a) ♠ A 4
  ♥ Q 9 7 4
  ♦ A Q 9 7 3
  ♣ 10 4

b) ♠ — *(5)*
  ♥ A J 8 5
  ♦ A Q 9 5 3   *17 pts*
  ♣ J 7 5 2

c) ♠ Q J 7 2
  ♥ Q J 5 4 .
  ♦ A K Q
  ♣ A 4

d) ♠ K 9 7 3
  ♥ 8 4
  ♦ A J 9 8 5
  ♣ A 7

e) ♠ Q 10 5
  ♥ 6 4
  ♦ K 10 8 7 5
  ♣ A K 8

f) ♠ K J 7
  ♥ Q 5
  ♦ A K Q 10 7
  ♣ K 10 5

g) ♠ Q 4
  ♥ 3
  ♦ K Q 9 7 5 · *CHIbACR*
  ♣ A Q 6 4 2

h) ♠ 8 3
  ♥ 6 3
  ♦ A Q 10 9 7 4
  ♣ A J 5

i) ♠ 5
  ♥ A 4
  ♦ K Q J 9 8 6 4
  ♣ K J 5

You open the bidding 1♣ and partner raises to 2♣.

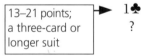

OPENER (YOU)	**RESPONDER (PARTNER)**
1♣	2♣

13–21 points;
a three-card or
longer suit

?   6–10 points;
club support

What do you rebid with each of the following hands?

j) ♠ A 10 7 3
  ♥ 6 4
  ♦ A Q 5
  ♣ Q J 8 4

k) ♠ Q 7
  ♥ K Q
  ♦ 4 3
  ♣ A Q J 7 6 4 2

l) ♠ A K J 7
  ♥ K Q 6
  ♦ K 8 4
  ♣ Q J 5

Answers to Quiz — Part II

a) 2♥. With support for responder's suit, value the hand using dummy points. There are 12 high-card points plus 1 point for each doubleton, a total of 14 valuation points. The hand is still a minimum opening bid, so raise to the cheapest level.

b) 3♥. Count 12 high-card points plus 5 dummy points for the void. The total of 17 valuation points puts the hand in the medium-strength opening bid category. Show the extra strength by making an invitational jump to the three level.

c) 4♥. There are 19 high-card points plus 1 dummy point for the doubleton club. That's enough to take the partnership to the game bonus level.

d) 1♠. There are 12 high-card points plus 1 length point. With no fit for responder's hearts, show the four-card spade suit.

e) 1NT. With no fit for hearts and no second suit to show at the one level, tell partner you have a balanced hand.

f) 2NT. A jump to 2NT shows a balanced hand too strong to start with 1NT.

g) 2♣. With an unbalanced hand, show the second suit.

h) 2♦. With no support for responder's suit and an unbalanced hand with no second suit to show, rebid the diamonds at the cheapest level.

i) 3♦. There are 14 high-card points plus 3 length points for the seven-card suit. Show a medium-strength opening by jumping a level when rebidding the suit.

j) Pass. You have 13 high-card points and responder has at most 10 for the raise to the two level.

k) 3♣. There are 14 high-card points plus 3 length points for the seven-card suit, a total of 17 valuation points. Make an invitational rebid, showing 17–18 points.

l) 3NT. This hand has 19 high-card points, putting it in the maximum-strength category for an opening bid. Even if responder has as few as 6 or 7 points, there should be enough combined strength for a game contract. 3NT requires only nine tricks.

Quiz – Part III

Partner opens 1♦ and you respond 1♠. Partner now raises to 2♠.

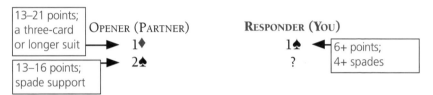

What call do you make with each of the following hands?

a) ♠ J 9 8 3
♥ A 3
♦ K 10 7 5
♣ 8 6 4

b) ♠ K 10 8 7 5 2
♥ Q 4
♦ A 9 2
♣ 9 6

c) ♠ A J 8 7 5
♥ 6 3
♦ Q 9 4
♣ A Q 5

How many sure tricks does declarer have in each of the following suits?
How could declarer try to get an extra trick?

d) DUMMY
♠ 7 5 4

e) DUMMY
♥ 8 4 2

f) DUMMY
♦ Q 6 3

g) DUMMY
♣ A K J

DECLARER
♠ K 8 2

DECLARER
♥ A Q

DECLARER
♦ A 7 4

DECLARER
♣ 7 5 3

East and West are defending against a spade contract and this is the layout
of the diamond suit. Would it be better if East or West led diamonds?

h)

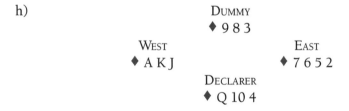

DUMMY
♦ 9 8 3

WEST
♦ A K J

EAST
♦ 7 6 5 2

DECLARER
♦ Q 10 4

Answers to Quiz — Part III

a) **Pass**. Opener's minimum raise shows a hand of about 13–16 points. You have 8 high-card points so the partnership belongs in partscore. You've found a fit in spades so there is no need to tell partner about the diamond support.

b) **3♠**. You have 9 high-card points plus 2 length points for a six-card suit. There could be enough combined strength for a game bonus. Raise to the three level and invite opener to continue to game with more than a bare minimum.

c) **4♠**. There are 13 high-card points plus 1 length point for the five-card suit. Opposite partner's opening bid, there should be enough for a game contract. You've discovered WHERE to play the contract. Let partner know How HIGH.

d) There are no sure tricks. Declarer can hope to get a trick by taking a finesse. Declarer must lead a spade from dummy toward the ♠K, hoping the ♠A is on declarer's right.

e) There is one sure trick. To get a second trick, declarer leads a heart from dummy and finesses the ♥Q, hoping the ♥K is on declarer's right. If the ♥K is on declarer's left, the finesse will lose and declarer will be back to one trick.

f) There is one sure trick. Declarer can take the ♦A and then lead toward dummy's ♦Q, hoping that the ♦K is favorably placed on declarer's left.

g) There are two sure tricks, the ♣A and ♣K. To get a third trick, declarer can lead a club toward dummy and finesse the ♣J. If the ♣Q is on declarer's left, the finesse will be successful.

h) **East**. The defenders want to arrange for East to lead through the strength in declarer's hand and up to the weakness in the dummy. The defenders can then take three diamond tricks. If West leads diamonds, West can take the first two tricks but declarer would then win the third round with the ♦Q. West doesn't want to lead through the weakness in dummy and up to the strength in declarer's hand. If East leads diamonds, the defenders are essentially taking a finesse against declarer's ♦Q.

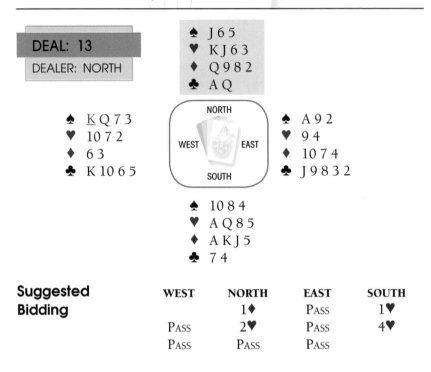

DEAL: 13
DEALER: NORTH

North:
- ♠ J 6 5
- ♥ K J 6 3
- ♦ Q 9 8 2
- ♣ A Q

West:
- ♠ K Q 7 3
- ♥ 10 7 2
- ♦ 6 3
- ♣ K 10 6 5

East:
- ♠ A 9 2
- ♥ 9 4
- ♦ 10 7 4
- ♣ J 9 8 3 2

South:
- ♠ 10 8 4
- ♥ A Q 8 5
- ♦ A K J 5
- ♣ 7 4

Suggested Bidding

WEST	NORTH	EAST	SOUTH
	1♦	PASS	1♥
PASS	2♥	PASS	4♥
PASS	PASS	PASS	

North has 13 high-card points, enough to open the bidding. Although the hand is balanced, it is too weak to open 1NT. There is no five-card or longer major suit so, North opens the bidding in the longer minor suit, diamonds.

East has only 5 high-card points plus 1 length point for the five-card suit. East passes.

South likes North's diamonds, but responder's priority is to look for a major suit fit. The diamond support can be shown later if no major suit fit is found. Responder can respond in a four-card major suit at the one level and bids 1♥. With 8 high-card points, West passes.

North has support for South's hearts but a minimum-strength opening bid. North describes this by raising to 2♥. North can't pass because South's bid in a new suit is forcing. East passes.

South now has to choose a rebid. Hearts have been agreed as a suitable trump suit, so the only decision is **HOW HIGH**. Since South has 14 high-card points, the partnership has enough combined strength for a game bonus. South jumps to 4♥. West, North, and East all pass. The contract is 4♥.

Suggested Opening Lead

South is declarer, so West makes the opening lead. Against a suit contract, the top of two touching cards can be led. West leads the ♠K.

Declarer's Plan

West leads and North puts the dummy on the table. South's goal is 10 tricks. There are four sure tricks in hearts, four in diamonds, and one in clubs. With a total of nine tricks, one more winner must be established.

South moves to the second planning stage and browses Declarer's Checklist. The only chance for a tenth trick is to make use of dummy's ♣Q with the help of a finesse. Declarer will have to hope that West holds the ♣K.

```
┌─ DECLARER'S PLAN—THE ABC'S ─┐

  Declarer: South    Contract: 4♥

  ASSESS THE SITUATION
  Goal                 10
  Sure Tricks           9
  Extra Tricks Needed   1

  BROWSE DECLARER'S CHECKLIST
  Promotion
  Length
  Finesse              1 in clubs
  Trumping in dummy

  CONSIDER THE ORDER
  • Draw trumps.
  • Be in the right place at the right
    time to lead toward dummy's ♣Q.
```

West's ♠K will win the first trick and East can make an encouraging signal by playing a high spade, the ♠9. West can continue leading spades and the defenders take the first three tricks. Suppose the defenders then lead a diamond or a heart.

Declarer wins this trick and can start by drawing trumps. This must be done so that the defenders can't trump any of the diamond winners. Once the defenders' trumps are drawn, it is safe to take the diamond winners. Eventually declarer needs to win a trick in the South hand and lead a club toward dummy's ♣A–Q. When West follows with a low club, declarer plays dummy's ♣Q. If West plays the ♣K, North takes it with the ♣A. East doesn't have the ♣K so the finesse works. Declarer now has 10 tricks.

If West leads a club early in the play, declarer can take the finesse at that point.

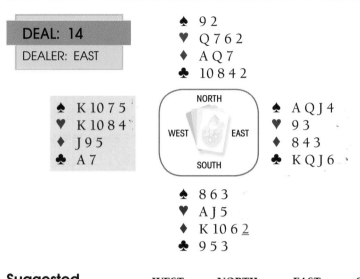

	♠	9 2
	♥	Q 7 6 2
	♦	A Q 7
	♣	10 8 4 2

DEAL: 14

DEALER: EAST

WEST		EAST
♠ K 10 7 5		♠ A Q J 4
♥ K 10 8 4		♥ 9 3
♦ J 9 5		♦ 8 4 3
♣ A 7		♣ K Q J 6

	♠	8 6 3
	♥	A J 5
	♦	K 10 6 2
	♣	9 5 3

Suggested Bidding

WEST	NORTH	EAST	SOUTH
		1♣	PASS
1♥	PASS	1♠	PASS
3♠	PASS	PASS	PASS

East has 13 high-card points and, with no five-card major suit, opens 1♣, the longer minor suit. South has only 8 high-card points and passes.

West, with 11 high-card points, has enough to respond. West's priority over East's minor suit opening bid is to look for a fit in a major suit. With a choice between the four-card heart suit and four-card spade suit, West bids up the line, lower-ranking four-card suit first. West responds 1♥.

With 8 high-card points, North passes.

East now has to choose a rebid. Responder's bid of a new suit, 1♥, is forcing. East doesn't have support for West's heart suit, but the search is still on for a major suit fit. East rebids 1♠.

South passes and West gets a chance to rebid. Since East has shown a four-card spade suit, an eight-card major suit fit has been found. West can value the hand as 11 high-card points plus 1 dummy point for the doubleton club. That's enough to make an invitational jump to 3♠. A raise to 2♠ would show about 6–10 points.

North passes and the auction returns to East. With a minimum for the opening bid, East passes. South passes and the auction is over. East becomes the declarer in a partscore contract of 3♠.

Suggested Opening Lead

South is on lead against the 3♠ contract. South might choose to lead a diamond, the only suit not bid by East-West. With no touching high cards, South would lead the ♦2, the fourth highest card.

Declarer's Plan

After the West hand comes down as the dummy, East makes a plan. As declarer, East's goal is to take at least nine tricks. East begins by counting the sure winners: four spades and four clubs for a total of eight tricks. One more trick is required.

Moving to the second stage, East browses Declarer's Checklist. The only possibility for an extra trick appears to be the ♥K. Declarer will have to hope that South holds the ♥A so that a successful finesse can be taken.

DECLARER'S PLAN—THE ABC'S

Declarer: East   Contract: 3♠

ASSESS THE SITUATION

Goal	9
Sure Tricks	8
Extra Tricks Needed	1

BROWSE DECLARER'S CHECKLIST

Promotion	
Length	
Finesse	1 in hearts
Trumping in dummy	

CONSIDER THE ORDER

- Draw trumps.
- High card from the short side first in clubs.
- Be in the right place at the right time to lead toward dummy's ♥K.

After South leads the ♦2, North will win the first trick with the ♦A and probably continue by leading the ♦Q. When this wins, North can lead a third diamond to South's ♦K. South might choose to lead a club at this point, hoping North holds the ♣K.

After winning a trick, declarer can start by drawing the defenders' trumps. This takes three rounds. Declarer can take the four club winners by winning the first trick with the ♣A, high card from the short side first. Then declarer is in the right place to lead a heart toward dummy's ♥K. If South wins the ♥A, dummy's ♥K is established as a winner when declarer regains the lead. If South doesn't play the ♥A, declarer can win a trick right away with dummy's ♥K.

DEAL: 15
DEALER: SOUTH

North:
- ♠ K 10 6
- ♥ A K 10 4
- ♦ 9 6 3
- ♣ 10 7 5

West:
- ♠ A 7 3
- ♥ 8 7 3
- ♦ A Q J 10 8 7
- ♣ A

East:
- ♠ Q 9 2
- ♥ J 5 2
- ♦ K 4
- ♣ 9 8 6 3 2

South:
- ♠ J 8 5 4
- ♥ Q 9 6
- ♦ 5 2
- ♣ K Q J 4

Suggested Bidding

WEST	NORTH	EAST	SOUTH
			Pass
1♦	Pass	1NT	Pass
3♦	Pass	Pass	Pass

South deals but, with 9 high-card points, does not have enough to open.

West has 15 high-card points plus 2 points for the six-card suit for a total of 17 valuation points. With an unbalanced hand, West opens the long suit, diamonds.

North has 10 high-card points and passes.

East has 6 high-card points plus 1 length point for the five-card suit. That's enough to respond. East doesn't have support for West's diamonds, doesn't have a four-card or longer suit that can be bid at the one level, and doesn't have enough strength to introduce a new suit at the two level. East is left with a response of 1NT.

South passes and West has to choose a rebid. With 17 points, West has a medium-strength opening bid and can show the extra length in diamonds and the extra strength by jumping to 3♦. A rebid of 2♦ would show a minimum opening. North passes.

East has another chance to bid. Although West has shown extra strength, East is minimum for the 1NT response and passes.

Suggested Opening Lead

North makes the opening lead. With touching honors in hearts, North starts with the ♥A, top of the touching high cards.

Declarer's Plan

West's goal is to take at least nine tricks. West can count on one trick from spades, six tricks from diamonds, and one sure trick in clubs. That's a total of eight tricks, one short of the goal.

West browses Declarer's Checklist for ways to develop the extra trick. Dummy's ♠Q presents a chance for a finesse. If North holds the ♠K, declarer can lead toward the ♠Q.

After winning the first trick with the ♥A, North will likely continue with the ♥K, espe-

---

┌─ DECLARER'S PLAN—THE ABC'S ─┐

Declarer: West   Contract: 3♦

ASSESS THE SITUATION
Goal	9
Sure Tricks	8
Extra Tricks Needed	1

BROWSE DECLARER'S CHECKLIST
Promotion	
Length	
Finesse	1 in spades
Trumping in dummy	

CONSIDER THE ORDER
- Draw trumps.
- High card from the short side first in diamonds.
- Be in the right place at the right time to lead toward dummy's ♠Q.

---

cially if South makes an encouraging signal by playing the ♥9, a high card, on the first trick. If North leads a third round of hearts, South will win with the ♥Q. South will then lead the ♣K, hoping to establish tricks for the defenders in that suit.

After winning a trick with the ♣A, declarer can start by drawing trumps. The first diamond trick can be won with dummy's ♦K, high card from the short side, and declarer can continue to lead diamonds until the defenders have none left.

Next it is time for the spade finesse. Declarer plays the ♠A and leads a low spade toward dummy's ♠Q. If North plays the ♠K, declarer plays low from dummy and later wins a trick with dummy's ♠Q; if North plays a low spade, declarer can win a trick right away.

If South held the ♠K, the finesse would not work, but declarer has no other way to get a ninth trick.

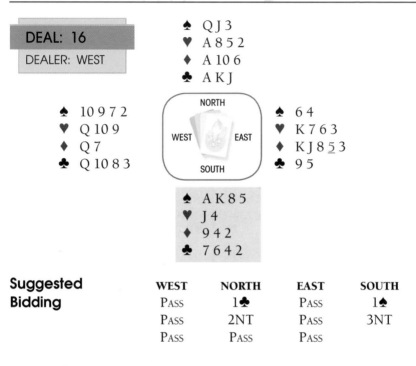

DEAL: 16

DEALER: WEST

NORTH

♠ Q J 3
♥ A 8 5 2
♦ A 10 6
♣ A K J

WEST

♠ 10 9 7 2
♥ Q 10 9
♦ Q 7
♣ Q 10 8 3

EAST

♠ 6 4
♥ K 7 6 3
♦ K J 8 5 3
♣ 9 5

SOUTH

♠ A K 8 5
♥ J 4
♦ 9 4 2
♣ 7 6 4 2

**Suggested
Bidding**

WEST	NORTH	EAST	SOUTH
PASS	1♣	PASS	1♠
PASS	2NT	PASS	3NT
PASS	PASS	PASS	

West is the dealer and, with only 6 high-card points, passes.

North has a balanced hand with 19 high-card points, too much to open 1NT. With no five-card major suit, North opens in a minor suit. With three cards in both diamonds and clubs, North opens 1♣.

East, with 7 high-card points plus 1 length point for the fifth diamond, passes. South has four-card support for North's clubs, but the priority is to look for a major suit fit, so South responds 1♠.

West passes and North has to choose a rebid. North describes a balanced hand too strong to open 1NT by jumping to 2NT. If North were to rebid only 1NT, that would show a hand too weak to open 1NT, about 13 or 14 points.

East passes and South chooses a rebid as responder. South has 8 high-card points and North has shown at least 18, so the partnership has enough combined strength for a game contract. Although South has support for clubs, South prefers the game contract of 3NT since that requires only nine tricks rather than eleven.

West, North, and East pass and North becomes declarer in 3NT.

Suggested Opening Lead

With no solid sequence, East chooses the fourth highest card from the long suit, the ♦5. East is hoping that the partnership can develop enough tricks in the diamond suit to defeat the contract.

Declarer's Plan

North is declarer and the goal is to take nine tricks in notrump. North counts four sure tricks in spades, one in hearts, one in diamonds, and two in clubs, for a total of eight. One more trick needs to be developed.

Browsing Declarer's Checklist, there is an opportunity to get an extra trick in the club suit with the help of a finesse. Declarer can hope West holds the ♣Q and plan to lead a club from the dummy toward the ♣J.

```
┌─ DECLARER'S PLAN—THE ABC'S ─┐

  Declarer: North   Contract: 3NT

  ASSESS THE SITUATION
  Goal                      9
  Sure Tricks               8
  Extra Tricks Needed       1

  BROWSE DECLARER'S CHECKLIST
  Promotion
  Length
  Finesse              1 in clubs
  Trumping in dummy

  CONSIDER THE ORDER
  • High cards from the short side first
    in spades.
  • Be in the right place at the right
    time to lead toward dummy's ♣J.
```

When East leads the ♦5, West should play the ♦Q, third hand high, trying to win the trick. North doesn't have to win the ♦A on the first round and may choose not to take it. In that case, West can return partner's suit, leading back the ♦7. If North refuses to win this trick, East will win and can lead a third round to drive out the ♦A.

After winning the ♦A, declarer can take the four spade winners starting with the high cards from the short side. North wins tricks with the ♠Q and ♠J and then plays the ♠3 over to dummy's ♠A and ♠K.

Declarer is now in the right hand to take the club finesse. A low club is led from dummy and, when West produces a low club, declarer finesses North's ♣J. Since East doesn't hold the ♣Q, the finesse succeeds and declarer has nine tricks.[23]

---

[23] Declarer can first play the ♣A or ♣K from the North hand just in case East holds a singleton ♣Q. On the actual deal, this won't make any difference.

Additional Practice Deals

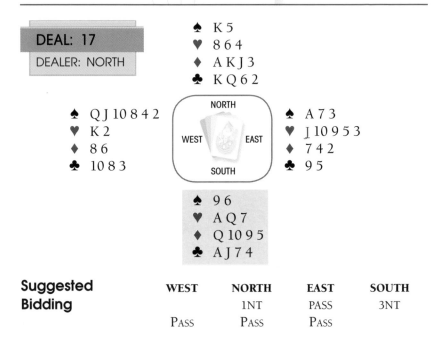

DEAL: 17
DEALER: NORTH

NORTH
♠ K 5
♥ 8 6 4
♦ A K J 3
♣ K Q 6 2

WEST
♠ Q J 10 8 4 2
♥ K 2
♦ 8 6
♣ 10 8 3

EAST
♠ A 7 3
♥ J 10 9 5 3
♦ 7 4 2
♣ 9 5

SOUTH
♠ 9 6
♥ A Q 7
♦ Q 10 9 5
♣ A J 7 4

Suggested Bidding

WEST	NORTH	EAST	SOUTH
	1NT	PASS	3NT
PASS	PASS	PASS	

North is the dealer and, with 16 high-card points and a balanced hand, opens the bidding 1NT.

East has 5 high-card points plus 1 length point for the five-card suit, not enough to enter the auction.

South, with 13 high-card points, and a balanced hand knows **How High**—game—and **Where**—notrump. South jumps to 3NT.

West has 6 high-card points plus 2 length points for the six-card suit, not enough to come into the auction.

North accepts responder's decision to play game in notrump and passes. East passes and the auction is over. North is declarer in a contract of 3NT.

Suggested Opening Lead

Since North is declarer, East makes the opening lead. With a solid sequence in hearts, East leads the ♥J, top of the solid sequence.

Declarer's Plan

South puts down the dummy hand and declarer makes a plan. North's goal is to take nine tricks in notrump.

North counts the sure tricks. There is one sure heart trick, the ♥A. There are four sure diamond winners and four sure club winners. That's a total of nine tricks, everything that is

---

DECLARER'S PLAN—THE ABC'S

Declarer: North   Contract: 3NT

ASSESS THE SITUATION
Goal	9
Sure Tricks	9
Extra Tricks Needed	0

BROWSE DECLARER'S CHECKLIST
- Not applicable

CONSIDER THE ORDER
- Take the tricks and run.

---

required. There's no need to look for extra tricks so North can take the tricks. The challenge is to resist the temptation to get an extra trick with the ♥Q.

If North doesn't count the sure tricks before deciding which card to play from dummy to the first trick, the contract might be defeated. If North chooses to play dummy's ♥Q on the first trick hoping East holds the ♥K, the finesse loses and West wins with the ♥K. West can now lead the ♠Q and declarer's ♠K is trapped. Whether or not declarer chooses to play the ♠K, the defenders can take six spade tricks to go with the ♥K, defeating the contract by three tricks.

Declarer doesn't need a trick with dummy's ♥Q, so taking the finesse only puts a safe contract at risk.

		♠ 10 9 5
DEAL: 18		♥ 9 8 7 4 3
DEALER: EAST		♦ J 9 5
		♣ 10 8

♠ K 8 2		NORTH		♠ A Q J
♥ K Q J 5	WEST		EAST	♥ 10 6
♦ Q 7 4				♦ A K 8 6 3
♣ 6 3 2		SOUTH		♣ A 7 4

♠ 7 6 4 3
♥ A 2
♦ 10 2
♣ <u>K</u> Q J 9 5

Suggested Bidding	WEST	NORTH	EAST	SOUTH
			1♦	PASS
	1♥	PASS	2NT	PASS
	3NT	PASS	PASS	PASS

East is the dealer and has 19 valuation points: 18 high-card points plus 1 length point for the five-card suit. Although the hand is balanced, it is too strong to open 1NT, so East opens 1♦, the longest suit.

South does not have the values to enter the auction at the two level by bidding 2♣. South passes.

West has 11 high-card points and, opposite East's 1♦ opening, the priority is to look for a major suit fit, so West responds 1♥.

North, with only 1 high-card point and 1 length point, passes.

East makes a rebid that describes the hand by jumping to 2NT. This shows a balanced hand of 18 or 19 points, too strong for 1NT.

South passes and West has to choose a rebid. With enough to take the partnership to the game contract in notrump, West bids 3NT.

North, East, and South pass and the auction is over.

Suggested Opening Lead

South, on declarer's left, is on lead against the 3NT contract. South leads the ♣K, top of the solid three-card sequence.

Declarer's Plan

West puts down the dummy and declarer makes a plan. East's goal is to take at least nine tricks. There are only three sure tricks in spades because there are three cards in each hand. There are three sure tricks in diamonds and one in clubs. Two more tricks are required.

East browses Declarer's Checklist. One possibility is to promote winners in hearts by driving out the defenders' ♥A.

```
┌─ DECLARER'S PLAN—THE ABC'S ─┐

Declarer: East     Contract: 3NT

ASSESS THE SITUATION
  Goal                    9
  Sure Tricks             7
  Extra Tricks Needed     2

BROWSE DECLARER'S CHECKLIST
  Promotion          3 in hearts
  Length             2 in diamonds
  Finesse
  Trumping in dummy

CONSIDER THE ORDER
  • Take the tricks and run—choose
    diamonds over hearts.
  • High card from the short side first
    in diamonds.
```

The danger is that when the defenders gain the lead with the ♥A, they may be able to take enough club winners to defeat the contract.

A second possibility is to take two extra tricks through length in the diamond suit. This will work if the five diamonds in the defenders' hands are divided 3-2. The advantage of this plan is that declarer doesn't have to give up the lead while taking the winners. Declarer can take the tricks and run. Also, if the diamonds don't divide 3-2, declarer can fall back on promoting winners in the heart suit . . . hoping the defenders can't take enough club tricks to defeat the contract after winning the ♥A.

After winning a trick with the ♣A[24], declarer plays a diamond to dummy's ♦Q—high card from the short side—and a diamond back to the ♦K. When both defenders follow suit, there is only one diamond outstanding. Declarer takes the ♦A and the remaining two diamonds are winners. Declarer then takes the three spade winners to make the contract without giving up the lead.

If declarer chose to promote winners in hearts instead of taking the diamond tricks, South could win the ♥A and take four club tricks to defeat the contract.

[24] Declarer might hold up winning the ♣A until the third round of the suit.

	♠ K 2
DEAL: 19	♥ K 10 4
DEALER: SOUTH	♦ 7 6 5 4 3
	♣ J 8 2

WEST		EAST
♠ 8 6 3	NORTH	♠ Q J 10 7 4
♥ 7 5 2	WEST ⬧ EAST	♥ 8 3
♦ 10 9	SOUTH	♦ Q J 8 2
♣ A K Q 6 3		♣ 10 7

♠ A 9 5
♥ A Q J 9 6
♦ A K
♣ 9 5 4

Suggested Bidding

WEST	NORTH	EAST	SOUTH
			1♥
PASS	2♥	PASS	4♥
PASS	PASS	PASS	

South is the dealer and values the hand as 19 points: 18 high-card points plus 1 length point for the five-card suit. With a five-card major suit, South opens 1♥.

West has 9 high-card points plus 1 length point for the five-card suit. West passes.

North has three-card support for South's hearts and raises to the appropriate level. With 7 high-card points plus 1 dummy point for the doubleton spade, North raises to the two level, showing the support and about 6–10 points.

East, with 6 high-card points plus 1 length point for the five-card suit, passes.

South has found a trump fit and, with a maximum-strength hand for opening at the one level, goes for the bonus by jumping to 4♥.

West, North, and East pass, ending the auction. South is declarer in a 4♥ contract and will have to take ten tricks.

Suggested Opening Lead

West, on declarer's left, makes the opening lead. With a solid sequence in clubs, West leads the ♣A, top of the touching high cards.

Declarer's Plan

After West leads, North puts down the dummy and declarer makes a plan. South's goal is to take ten tricks. There are two sure spade winners, five hearts, and two diamonds. One more trick is needed.

Declarer browses the checklist. In the spade suit, declarer has more spades than the dummy. This presents an opportunity to trump a spade in dummy for declarer's tenth trick.

In considering the order, however, declarer must be careful to leave a trump in the dummy with which to ruff the spade. That means declarer can't afford to draw all the defenders' trumps right away.

DECLARER'S PLAN—THE ABC'S

Declarer: South   Contract: 4♥

ASSESS THE SITUATION
Goal	10
Sure Tricks	9
Extra Tricks Needed	1

BROWSE DECLARER'S CHECKLIST
Promotion
Length
Finesse
Trumping in dummy   1 in spades

CONSIDER THE ORDER
- Draw trumps but . . .
- Keep a trump in dummy to ruff a spade.
- Develop the extra trick in spades early.
- High card from the short side first in spades.

Suppose West takes the first three club tricks and then leads a diamond. Declarer wins this trick and can afford to draw two rounds of trumps but must then turn attention to the spades. Declarer plays a spade to dummy's ♠K—high card from the short side – and a spade back to the ♠A. Now declarer leads the remaining spade and trumps it in the dummy.

Declarer can then return to the South hand with a diamond winner and draw the outstanding trump. Declarer has the rest of the tricks and North-South get a game bonus for bidding and making 4♥.

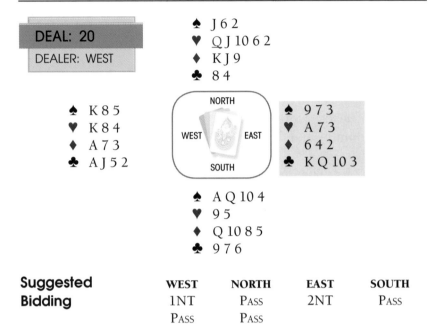

DEAL: 20

DEALER: WEST

NORTH
♠ J 6 2
♥ Q J 10 6 2
♦ K J 9
♣ 8 4

WEST
♠ K 8 5
♥ K 8 4
♦ A 7 3
♣ A J 5 2

EAST
♠ 9 7 3
♥ A 7 3
♦ 6 4 2
♣ K Q 10 3

SOUTH
♠ A Q 10 4
♥ 9 5
♦ Q 10 8 5
♣ 9 7 6

Suggested	**WEST**	**NORTH**	**EAST**	**SOUTH**
Bidding	1NT	Pass	2NT	Pass
	Pass	Pass		

West is the dealer with 15 valuation points, all in high cards, and a balanced hand. West opens the bidding 1NT.

North has 8 high-card points plus 1 length point for the five-card suit, not enough to enter the auction.

East has 9 high-card points and a balanced hand. East decides **How High** and **Where**. East knows **Where**, notrump. The partnership may have enough strength for the game bonus if West has the top of the 1NT range, but the partnership may belong in partscore if opener has the bottom of the range. East invites West to game in notrump by raising to 2NT.

South has 8 high-card points and passes.

West, with only 15 points, the bottom of the range for the 1NT opening, passes, rejecting the invitation and settling for partscore.

North passes and the auction is over. West is declarer in 2NT.

Suggested Opening Lead

North, to declarer's left, makes the opening lead. North leads the ♥Q, top of the sequence in that suit.

Declarer's Plan

The East hand comes down as the dummy and declarer makes a plan. West's goal is to take eight tricks.

West counts the sure tricks. There are two heart tricks, one diamond, and four club tricks. One more trick is required.

Declarer browses the checklist. The only chance for an eighth winner is to get a trick with the ♠K. This can be done with the help of a finesse if South holds the ♠A. Declarer must plan to lead toward the ♠K.

> ### DECLARER'S PLAN—THE ABC'S
>
> Declarer: West   Contract: 2NT
>
> **ASSESS THE SITUATION**
> | | |
> |---|---|
> | Goal | 8 |
> | Sure Tricks | 7 |
> | Extra Tricks Needed | 1 |
>
> **BROWSE DECLARER'S CHECKLIST**
> | | |
> |---|---|
> | Promotion | |
> | Length | |
> | Finesse | 1 in spades |
> | Trumping in dummy | |
>
> **CONSIDER THE ORDER**
> - Develop the extra spade trick early.
> - Be in the right place at the right time to lead toward dummy's ♠K.

Declarer has to lead a spade from the dummy and wants to do so while still retaining winners in the other suits with which to regain the lead. There's not much point in delaying the finesse, so declarer can win the first trick with dummy's ♥A and lead a spade right away.

If South takes the ♠A, declarer's ♠K has become a winner. On regaining the lead, declarer has eight tricks. If South doesn't play the ♠A right away, declarer plays the ♠K and wins the trick. Declarer takes the remaining heart winner, the ♦A, and four club tricks to make the contract.

If North held the ♠A, the finesse would lose and the contract would be defeated. Declarer has to hope that the ♠A is favorably located in the South hand.

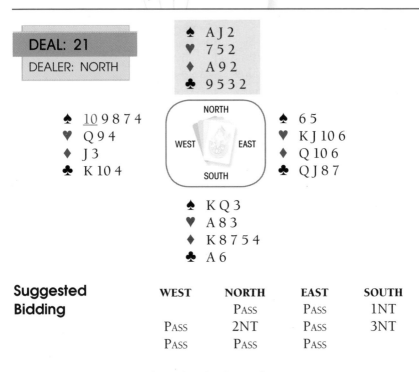

♠ A J 2
♥ 7 5 2
♦ A 9 2
♣ 9 5 3 2

♠ 10 9 8 7 4
♥ Q 9 4
♦ J 3
♣ K 10 4

NORTH

WEST   EAST

SOUTH

♠ 6 5
♥ K J 10 6
♦ Q 10 6
♣ Q J 8 7

♠ K Q 3
♥ A 8 3
♦ K 8 7 5 4
♣ A 6

Suggested	WEST	NORTH	EAST	SOUTH
Bidding		P̴ass	P̴ass	1NT
	P̴ass	2NT	P̴ass	3NT
	P̴ass	P̴ass	P̴ass	

North is the dealer and, with 9 high-card points, passes.

East has 9 high-card points and also passes.

South has 16 high-card points plus 1 length point for the five-card suit and a balanced hand. South opens the bidding 1NT.

West, with 6 high-card points plus 1 length point for the five-card suit, passes.

North, with 9 high-card points, knows **Where**, notrump, but can't be sure **How High**. The partnership may have enough combined strength for the game bonus. North makes an invitational response to South's 1NT opening by raising to 2NT.

East passes and South has to make a rebid. With a maximum for 1NT, South accepts North's invitation by continuing to game.

West, North, and East pass. South is declarer in a 3NT contract.

Suggested Opening Lead

Since South is declarer, West makes the opening lead. With a solid sequence in spades, West leads the ♠10, top of the sequence.

Declarer's Plan

North puts the dummy hand face up on the table and declarer makes a plan. South's goal is to take nine tricks in notrump.

South counts the sure tricks. There are three sure spade tricks, one heart, two diamonds, and one club. That's a total of seven tricks. Two more tricks are needed.

Declarer browses the checklist for developing additional tricks. The diamond suit offers a chance for developing the

```
┌─── DECLARER'S PLAN—THE ABC'S ───┐
│ Declarer: South   Contract: 3NT     │
│ ASSESS THE SITUATION                 │
│   Goal                    9          │
│   Sure Tricks             7          │
│   Extra Tricks Needed   2            │
│                                      │
│ BROWSE DECLARER'S CHECKLIST          │
│   Promotion                          │
│   Length              2 in diamonds  │
│   Finesse                            │
│   Trumping in dummy                  │
│                                      │
│ CONSIDER THE ORDER                   │
│   • Develop the extra diamond tricks │
│     early.                           │
└──────────────────────────────────────┘
```

two extra tricks through length. North-South have eight combined diamonds, leaving five for East-West. If the missing diamonds are divided 3-2, two diamond winners can be established by giving one trick to the defenders.

Considering the order, declarer wants to develop the diamond tricks early while still having control of the other suits. After winning the first spade trick, declarer takes a trick with the ♦A, a trick with the ♦K, and leads a third round of the suit, giving a trick to the defenders.

After East wins the third round of diamonds, it doesn't matter which suit East leads. Declarer wins and can take the two established diamond tricks and the remaining winners. That's nine tricks and North-South get a game bonus.

If declarer were to take the seven sure tricks and then give up a diamond trick, the contract can be defeated. The defenders will have enough established winners to take the rest of the tricks.

DEAL: 22	♠ 8 4 2
DEALER: EAST	♥ Q J 10 4
	♦ 9 5
	♣ A J 6 3

		NORTH		
♠ Q J 10 5				♠ A K 9 3
♥ 9 8 5	WEST		EAST	♥ 6 3 2
♦ K 7 4 2				♦ A 8 6 3
♣ K 8		SOUTH		♣ Q 9

♠ 7 6
♥ A K 7
♦ Q J 10
♣ 10 7 5 4 2

Suggested Bidding	WEST	NORTH	EAST	SOUTH
			1♦	Pass
	1♠	Pass	2♠	Pass
	Pass	Pass		

East is the dealer and has 13 valuation points, all in high-card points. Although the hand is balanced, it is not strong enough to open 1NT. With no five-card major suit, East opens 1♦, the longer minor suit.

South has 10 high-card points and 1 length point for the five-card suit, not enough to enter the auction at the two level.

West has 9 high-card points, enough to respond. Although West has support for East's diamonds, the priority is to look for a major suit fit. West responds 1♠, showing four or more spades and 6 or more points.

North has 8 high-card points and passes.

West's response in a new suit is forcing, so East can't pass. With support for West's spades, East can raise to the appropriate level. With a minimum opening bid, East raises to 2♠, the cheapest level.

South passes and West has to decide what to do next. Since East has shown a minimum-strength opening bid of 13–16 points, the partnership is unlikely to have enough combined strength for a game bonus. Having found the spade fit, West passes and stops in partscore.

North passes, ending the auction. West will be declarer in the 2♠ contract.

Suggested Opening Lead

North, on declarer's left, is on lead against the 2♠ contract. North leads the ♥Q, top of the solid three-card sequence.

Declarer's Plan

East puts down the dummy and declarer makes a plan. West's goal is to take at least eight tricks. There are four sure trick in spades and two in diamonds. Two more tricks are required.

West browses Declarer's Checklist. One extra trick can be developed in clubs through promotion. Declarer can use a high club to drive out the defenders' ♣A, promoting the other club into a winner. The

```
┌─── DECLARER'S PLAN—THE ABC'S ───┐
│ Declarer: West      Contract: 2♠     │
│                                       │
│ ASSESS THE SITUATION                  │
│   Goal                    8           │
│   Sure Tricks             6           │
│   Extra Tricks Needed     2           │
│                                       │
│ BROWSE DECLARER'S CHECKLIST           │
│   Promotion          1 in clubs       │
│   Length             1 in diamonds    │
│   Finesse                             │
│   Trumping in dummy                   │
│                                       │
│ CONSIDER THE ORDER                    │
│   • Draw trumps first.                │
│   • Develop the extra tricks early.   │
└───────────────────────────────────────┘
```

diamond suit offers a chance to develop a trick through length if the five missing diamonds are divided 3-2, as might be expected.

Suppose the defenders take the first three heart tricks and then lead a diamond. Declarer wins this trick and the first task is to draw trumps. This can done in three rounds. Then declarer can promote a club winner.

Suppose North wins the ♣A and leads another club. Declarer wins and next establishes an extra trick in diamonds by taking the remaining high diamond and giving a trick to the defenders. It doesn't matter what the defenders lead next, declarer has the remaining tricks with a trump and an established diamond winner.

Declarer loses three heart tricks, the ♣A, and a diamond trick, but finishes with eight tricks, just enough to make the contract.

DEAL: 23

DEALER: SOUTH

♠ K J 10 9 7 3
♥ 5 3
♦ J 6 3
♣ A 4

NORTH

WEST   EAST

SOUTH

♠ A 8 5
♥ Q 4
♦ A 9 7
♣ 10 7 6 5 3

♠ 6 2
♥ K 10 9 8
♦ K 8 4 2
♣ Q J 9

♠ Q 4
♥ A J 7 6 2
♦ Q 10 5
♣ K 8 2

Suggested Bidding

WEST	NORTH	EAST	SOUTH
			1♥
PASS	1♠	PASS	1NT
PASS	3♠	PASS	PASS
PASS			

South is the dealer and values the hand as 13 points: 12 high-card points plus 1 length point for the five-card suit. With a five-card major suit, South opens 1♥.

West has 10 high-card points plus 1 length point for the five-card suit. That's not enough to suggest the club suit as trumps at the two level. West passes.

North has 9 high-card points plus 2 length points for the six-card suit. Without support for South's hearts, North bids 1♠, showing 6 or more points and four or more spades.

East has 9 high-card points and passes.

South doesn't have support for North's spades and must find a descriptive rebid since North's response in a new suit is forcing. Having already shown the five-card heart suit, South can show a balanced hand by rebidding 1NT. This shows a balanced hand too weak to open 1NT originally.

West passes and the auction comes back to North. From the 1NT rebid, North knows that South has at least two spades—otherwise, South would not have a balanced hand. The partnership has an eight-card fit in the major. With 11 points, North can make an invitational jump to 3♠, inviting partner to bid game.

Easts passes. South passes with a bare minimum for the opening bid, turning down the invitation.

Suggested Opening Lead

East makes the opening lead. Since South bid hearts, East probably doesn't want to lead that suit. East might choose the ♣Q.

Declarer's Plan

After East leads, South puts down the dummy and North makes a plan. The goal is to take nine tricks. There is one sure heart trick and two club tricks. Six more tricks are needed.

Declarer browses the checklist. Declarer can plan to promote five winners in the spade suit by driving out the ♠A. In

---

DECLARER'S PLAN—THE ABC'S

Declarer: North   Contract: 3♠

ASSESS THE SITUATION

Goal	9
Sure Tricks	3
Extra Tricks Needed	6

BROWSE DECLARER'S CHECKLIST

Promotion	5 in spades
	1 in diamonds
Length	
Finesse	
Trumping in dummy	

CONSIDER THE ORDER

- Draw trumps first.
- High card from the short side first in spades.
- Develop the extra diamond trick early.

---

addition, a winner can be promoted in the diamond suit by driving out both the defenders' ♦A and ♦K.

After winning the first club trick, declarer starts promoting winners in the trump suit. Declarer should start with the ♠Q, high card from the short side. Suppose the defenders win the ♠A and lead another club. Declarer wins and continues leading spades until all the defenders trumps are drawn. This takes two more rounds.

Now declarer goes about promoting a diamond winner. Declarer leads a high diamond to drive out the ♦K. On regaining the lead, declarer leads another high diamond to drive out the ♦A. Declarer's remaining high diamond is now a winner.

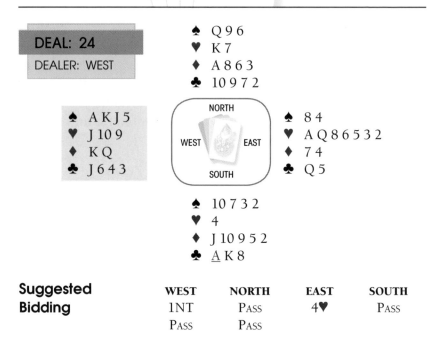

	♠	Q 9 6
	♥	K 7
	♦	A 8 6 3
	♣	10 9 7 2

DEAL: 24
DEALER: WEST

♠ A K J 5		♠ 8 4
♥ J 10 9		♥ A Q 8 6 5 3 2
♦ K Q		♦ 7 4
♣ J 6 4 3		♣ Q 5

	♠	10 7 3 2
	♥	4
	♦	J 10 9 5 2
	♣	A K 8

**Suggested
Bidding**

WEST	NORTH	EAST	SOUTH
1NT	PASS	4♥	PASS
PASS	PASS		

West is the dealer and, with 15 valuation points and a balanced hand, opens the bidding 1NT.

North has 9 high-card points and passes.

East has a seven-card heart suit and knows West has at least two hearts for the 1NT opening bid. That decides the question of **WHERE**. East has 8 high-card points plus 3 length points for the seven-card suit. The partnership must have at least 26 combined points, so that decides the question of **HOW HIGH**, game. East takes the partnership directly to a game contract with hearts as the trump suit by jumping to 4♥.

South, West, and North all pass, ending the auction. The contract is 4♥ and East is the declarer.

Suggested Opening Lead

South, to declarer's left, makes the opening lead. South leads the ♣A, top of the touching cards in that suit.

Declarer's Plan

After South makes the opening lead, the West hand comes down as the dummy and declarer makes a plan. East's goal is to take ten tricks.

East counts the sure tricks. There are two spade tricks and one heart. Seven more tricks are needed.

East browses Declarer's Checklist. One winner can be promoted in the diamond suit, but the remaining winners will have to come from the heart suit. Declarer needs to take all seven tricks in the heart suit. In addition to the ♥A, five extra tricks will come through promotion and length. However, one extra trick will require the use of the finesse.

Suppose South wins the first two club tricks and then leads a diamond. North takes the ♦A and then leads another diamond which is won in the West hand, the dummy. Declarer needs the rest of the tricks. The only real chance is that North holds the ♥K. Declarer leads the ♥J from dummy and, if North plays a low heart, takes the finesse by playing a low heart. Fortunately, North holds the ♥K and the finesse succeeds. Declarer makes the contract. If the finesse had lost to the ♥K in the South hand, the contract would be defeated.

DECLARER'S PLAN—THE ABC'S

Declarer: East   Contract: 4♥

ASSESS THE SITUATION

Goal	10
Sure Tricks	3
Extra Tricks Needed	7

BROWSE DECLARER'S CHECKLIST

Promotion	1 in diamonds
Length	5 in hearts
Finesse	1 in hearts
Trumping in dummy	

CONSIDER THE ORDER

- Draw trumps.
- Be in the right place at the right time to lead the ♥J from dummy.

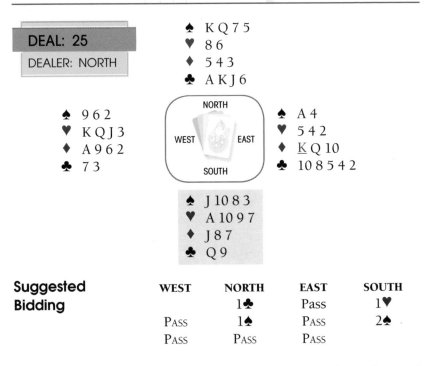

	North		
	♠ K Q 7 5		
	♥ 8 6		
	♦ 5 4 3		
	♣ A K J 6		

DEAL: 25

DEALER: NORTH

West
♠ 9 6 2
♥ K Q J 3
♦ A 9 6 2
♣ 7 3

East
♠ A 4
♥ 5 4 2
♦ K Q 10
♣ 10 8 5 4 2

South
♠ J 10 8 3
♥ A 10 9 7
♦ J 8 7
♣ Q 9

Suggested Bidding

WEST	NORTH	EAST	SOUTH
	1♣	Pass	1♥
Pass	1♠	Pass	2♠
Pass	Pass	Pass	

North is the dealer and has 13 high-card points. With no five-card major suit, North opens 1♣, the longer minor suit.

East has 9 high-card points plus 1 length point and passes.

South has 8 high-card points, enough to respond to North's opening bid. The priority is to look for a major suit fit. With four cards in both majors, South responds "up the line", bidding the first four-card suit encountered when going up the Bidding Ladder.

West has 10 high-card points and passes.

North can't support South's major, but there is still room at the one level to continue searching for a major suit fit. North bids 1♠.

East passes and South has support for opener's second suit. To show the support and a minimum response, South raises to 2♠.

West passes. North has nothing extra and passes. East passes and the auction is over. North is declarer in a partscore contract of 2♠.

Suggested Opening Lead

Since North is declarer, East makes the opening lead. Since the opponents have bid clubs, hearts, and spades, East chooses the unbid suit, diamonds. East leads the ♦K, top of the touching high cards.

Declarer's Plan

East makes the opening lead and South puts down the dummy. Declarer makes a plan. North's goal is to take eight tricks with spades as trumps.

North counts the sure tricks. There is one heart trick and four club winners. Three more tricks need to be developed.

North browses Declarer's Checklist. The spade suit can provide the three required tricks through promotion. A trick must be lost to the ♠A,

---

┌─ DECLARER'S PLAN—THE ABC'S ─┐

Declarer: North   Contract: 2♠

ASSESS THE SITUATION
Goal	8
Sure Tricks	5
Extra Tricks Needed	3

BROWSE DECLARER'S CHECKLIST
Promotion	3 in spades
Length	
Finesse	
Trumping in dummy	

CONSIDER THE ORDER
- Draw trumps first.
- Promote extra spade tricks early.
- High card from the short side first in clubs.

---

but that's all. Declarer will then be able to draw the remaining trumps in the defenders' hands.

Suppose the defenders take the first three diamond tricks and lead a heart. Declarer wins the ♥A and immediately leads a high spade. Declarer wants to drive out the ♠A and draw trumps before taking the club winners. That will make sure the defenders can't trump one of the club winners.

Suppose the defenders win the ♠A and take their established heart winner and play another heart. Declarer trumps and draws the remaining trumps which takes two more rounds. Now it is safe for declarer to take the club winners. Declarer starts with the ♣Q, high card from the short side, and then plays a low club to the three remaining winners.

Declarer has eight tricks: three spades, one heart, and four clubs. That's enough to make the partscore contract of 2♠.

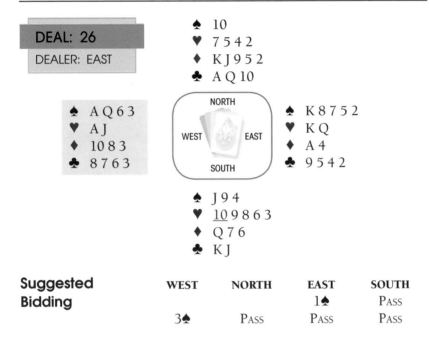

DEAL: 26
DEALER: EAST

NORTH
♠ 10
♥ 7 5 4 2
♦ K J 9 5 2
♣ A Q 10

WEST
♠ A Q 6 3
♥ A J
♦ 10 8 3
♣ 8 7 6 3

EAST
♠ K 8 7 5 2
♥ K Q
♦ A 4
♣ 9 5 4 2

SOUTH
♠ J 9 4
♥ 10 9 8 6 3
♦ Q 7 6
♣ K J

Suggested Bidding	WEST	NORTH	EAST	SOUTH
			1♠	PASS
	3♠	PASS	PASS	PASS

East is the dealer and has 13 valuation points: 12 high-card points plus 1 length point. East opens in the five-card major suit.

South has 7 high-card points and 1 length point for the five-card suit, not enough to enter the auction.

West has 11 high-card points and, with support for opener's major, can add 1 dummy point for the doubleton heart. To show the strength and support for East's spades, West jumps to 3♠, inviting opener to continue to game with a little extra.

North has 10 high-card points plus 1 length point for the five-card suit. The auction is already at the three level, so North passes.

West's jump raise shows four-card support and 11-12 points. East has a minimum opening with nothing extra. East turns down the invitation by passing. South passes and the auction is complete.

Suggested Opening Lead

South is on declarer's left and makes the opening lead. South leads the ♥10, top of the solid three-card sequence.

Declarer's Plan

West puts down the dummy and declarer makes a plan. East's goal is to take at least nine tricks. There are three sure tricks in spades, two in hearts, and one in diamonds. Three more tricks are required.

East browses Declarer's Checklist. The spade suit should provide two extra tricks through length. There are only four spades missing. If the missing spades divide 2-2 or, as is more likely, 3-1, declarer can draw all the defenders' spades with the top three winners in the suit. Declarer's remaining spades will be winners.

```
┌─── DECLARER'S PLAN—THE ABC'S ───┐
│ Declarer: East      Contract: 3♠ │
│                                   │
│ ASSESS THE SITUATION              │
│   Goal                    9       │
│   Sure Tricks             6       │
│   Extra Tricks Needed     3       │
│                                   │
│ BROWSE DECLARER'S CHECKLIST       │
│   Promotion                       │
│   Length              2 in spades │
│     1 in clubs                    │
│   Finesse                         │
│   Trumping in dummy               │
│                                   │
│ CONSIDER THE ORDER                │
│   • Draw trumps first.            │
│   • Develop the extra trick early.│
└───────────────────────────────────┘
```

The other possible source of a trick is the club suit. Although declarer has no high cards in the suit, a trick can be developed through length if the missing clubs are divided 3-2.

After winning the first heart trick, declarer's first task is to draw the outstanding trumps. This takes three rounds when the missing spades are divided 3-1.

Once the trumps are drawn, declarer develops the extra tricks early by going after clubs. Declarer plays a club and lets the opponents win the trick. Suppose the defenders lead another heart. Declarer wins and plays a second round of clubs, giving up another trick. Suppose the defenders now lead a diamond. Declarer wins the ♦A and plays a third round of clubs, giving up yet another trick.

All this hard work has paid off because declarer's remaining club is a winner. The defenders can take their diamond trick, but declarer's remaining cards are all winners. The only tricks declarer loses are a diamond and three clubs.

Declarer could not make the contract by taking all the winners before leading a club. The defenders could take their diamond and heart winners and declarer would have no way to regain the lead.

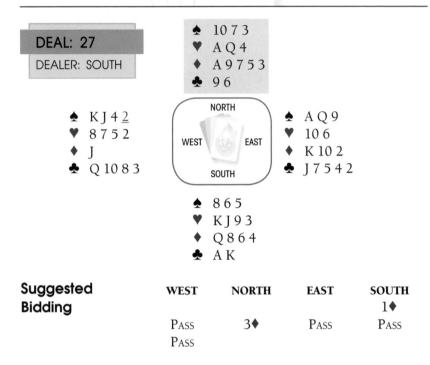

	DEAL: 27	♠ 10 7 3	
	DEALER: SOUTH	♥ A Q 4	
		♦ A 9 7 5 3	
		♣ 9 6	

♠ K J 4 2
♥ 8 7 5 2
♦ J
♣ Q 10 8 3

♠ A Q 9
♥ 10 6
♦ K 10 2
♣ J 7 5 4 2

♠ 8 6 5
♥ K J 9 3
♦ Q 8 6 4
♣ A K

Suggested Bidding	WEST	NORTH	EAST	SOUTH
				1♦
	Pass	3♦	Pass	Pass
	Pass			

South is the dealer and values the hand as 13 points, all in high cards. With no five-card major suit, South opens 1♦, the longer minor.

West has 7 high-card points and passes.

North has 10 high-card points plus 1 length point for the five-card suit. North doesn't have a four-card or longer major suit to bid but does have support for South's diamonds. A raise to the two level would show only 6-10 points, so North makes an invitational jump raise to the three level, showing 11-12 points.

East has 10 high-card points and 1 length point for the five-card suit. That isn't enough to enter the auction, so East passes.

South doesn't have anything extra for the opening bid and settles for partscore by passing. There's no point in bidding hearts since North would have responded 1♥ with a four-card or longer suit.

West passes and the auction is finished.

Suggested Opening Lead

West, on declarer's left, makes the opening lead. West might lead any of the unbid suits. Since the spades are strongest, West might choose the ♠2, fourth highest since there are no touching high cards in the suit.

Declarer's Plan

After West's opening lead, North puts down the dummy and declarer makes a plan. South's goal is to take nine tricks. There are four sure heart tricks, one diamond, and two club tricks. Two more tricks are needed.

Declarer browses the checklist. Declarer can plan to develop extra winners in the diamond suit through a combination of length and the finesse. There are four missing diamonds. Declarer can hope that the missing diamonds are divided 2-2 or, if they are divided 3-1, that East holds the ♦K.

DECLARER'S PLAN—THE ABC'S

Declarer: South   Contract: 3♦

ASSESS THE SITUATION

Goal	9
Sure Tricks	7
Extra Tricks Needed	2

BROWSE DECLARER'S CHECKLIST

Promotion	
Length	1 in diamonds
Finesse	1 in diamonds
Trumping in dummy	

CONSIDER THE ORDER

- Draw trumps first.
- Develop the extra tricks early.
- Be in the right place at the right time to lead toward the ♦Q.

Suppose the defenders take the first three spade tricks and then lead a club. Declarer wins and should immediately go after diamonds, the trump suit. Declarer plays the ♦A and then leads a diamond from dummy toward the ♦Q. Although the missing diamonds divide 3-1, declarer loses only one trick in the suit because East holds the ♦K. When a low diamond is led from dummy, if East takes the ♦K, South's ♦Q becomes a winner. On regaining the lead, declarer can draw the outstanding diamond and the remaining diamonds are all winners. If East doesn't take the ♦K, South can play the ♦Q, which wins the trick.

The only tricks lost by declarer are the three spade tricks and one diamond trick. North-South make the partscore contract of 3♦.

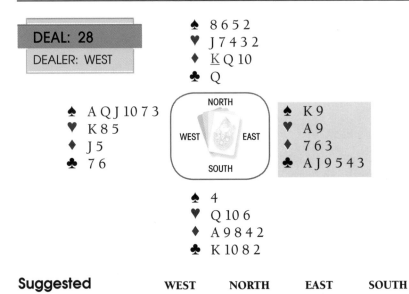

DEAL: 28
DEALER: WEST

♠ 8 6 5 2
♥ J 7 4 3 2
♦ K Q 10
♣ Q

♠ A Q J 10 7 3
♥ K 8 5
♦ J 5
♣ 7 6

NORTH
WEST   EAST
SOUTH

♠ K 9
♥ A 9
♦ 7 6 3
♣ A J 9 5 4 3

♠ 4
♥ Q 10 6
♦ A 9 8 4 2
♣ K 10 8 2

Suggested Bidding	**WEST**	**NORTH**	**EAST**	**SOUTH**
	1♠	Pass	2♣	Pass
	2♠	Pass	4♠	Pass
	Pass	Pass		

West is the dealer and has 13 valuation points: 11 high-card points plus 2 length points for the six-card suit. West opens the bidding 1♠, the six-card major suit.

North has 8 high-card points plus a length point for the five-card suit. That's not enough to come into the auction and North passes.

East has 12 high-card points plus 2 length points for the six-card suit. That's enough to bid a new suit at the two level and East responds 2♣ to West's opening 1♠ bid.

South has 9 high-card points plus 1 length point for the five-card suit. South passes.

East's response in a new suit is forcing and West has to make a descriptive rebid. With two doubletons, West's hand is unbalanced. West shows the extra length in the spade suit by rebidding 2♠.

North passes and East has to decide what call to make. Since West bid spades twice, the partnership should have at least an eight-card fit. East also knows the partnership has enough combined strength to go for a game, so East puts the partnership in 4♠.

Suggested Opening Lead

North, on declarer's left, makes the opening lead. North will likely pick one of the unbid suits, hearts or diamonds. With the sequence in diamonds, that suit appears to be the best choice. North leads the ♦K, top of the touching cards.

Declarer's Plan

After North leads, the East hand comes down as the dummy and declarer makes a plan. West's goal is to take ten tricks.

West counts the sure tricks. There are six spade tricks, two hearts, and one club. One more trick is needed.

West browses Declarer's Checklist. Since there are more hearts in declarer's hand than in the dummy, West can plan to ruff a heart in the dummy.

In considering the order, declarer has to make sure that

DECLARER'S PLAN—THE ABC'S

Declarer: West   Contract: 4♠

ASSESS THE SITUATION

Goal	10
Sure Tricks	9
Extra Tricks Needed	1

BROWSE DECLARER'S CHECKLIST

Promotion
Length
Finesse
Trumping in dummy   1 in hearts

CONSIDER THE ORDER

- Draw trumps but . . .
- Keep a trump in dummy to ruff a heart.
- Develop the extra heart trick early.

---

there is a spade left in the dummy with which to trump the heart. That means declarer will have to delay drawing all the trumps.

Suppose the defenders take the first two diamonds and lead a third round which declarer trumps. Before drawing all the trumps, declarer plays a heart to dummy's ♥A, a heart back to the ♥K, and a third round of hearts which is trumped in dummy.

Now declarer can draw the remaining trumps and has ten tricks: six spades plus the heart ruff in the dummy, two hearts, and the ♣A.

East-West get the game bonus for bidding and making 4♠.

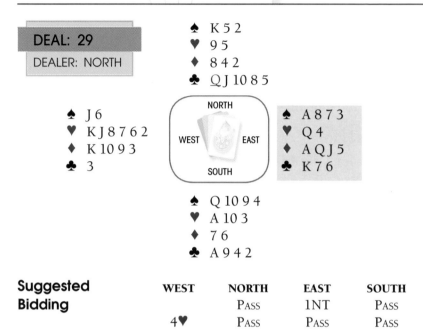

DEAL: 29
DEALER: NORTH

NORTH
♠ K 5 2
♥ 9 5
♦ 8 4 2
♣ Q J 10 8 5

WEST
♠ J 6
♥ K J 8 7 6 2
♦ K 10 9 3
♣ 3

EAST
♠ A 8 7 3
♥ Q 4
♦ A Q J 5
♣ K 7 6

SOUTH
♠ Q 10 9 4
♥ A 10 3
♦ 7 6
♣ A 9 4 2

Suggested Bidding

WEST	NORTH	EAST	SOUTH
	PASS	1NT	PASS
4♥	PASS	PASS	PASS

North is the dealer and has 6 high-card points plus 1 length point for the five-card suit, That isn't enough to open the bidding.

East has 16 high-card points and a balanced hand. That falls into the range for a 1NT opening bid.

South has 10 high-card points, not enough to enter the auction.

West considers **How High** and **Where** the partnership belongs. West has 8 high-card points plus 2 length points for the six-card suit. That's enough to go for the game bonus opposite a 1NT opening bid. So, West has the answer to **How High**, game. With a six-card major suit, West also has the answer to **Where**, hearts. East must have at least two hearts to show a balanced hand. So, West puts the partnership in a game contract of 4♥.

North, East, and South pass, ending the auction.

Suggested Opening Lead

Since West is declarer, North makes the opening lead. North leads the ♣Q, top of the solid sequence.

Declarer's Plan

After North makes the opening lead, East puts down the dummy. Declarer makes a plan. West's goal is to take ten tricks with hearts as the trump suit.

West counts the sure tricks. There is one spade trick and four diamond winners. Five more tricks need to be developed.

West browses Declarer's Checklist. The heart suit can provide the five extra tricks through a combination of promotion and length. Once the

┌─ DECLARER'S PLAN—THE ABC'S ─┐
Declarer: West Contract: 4♥
ASSESS THE SITUATION
Goal 10
Sure Tricks 5
Extra Tricks Needed 5
BROWSE DECLARER'S CHECKLIST
Promotion 2 in hearts
Length 3 in hearts
Finesse
Trumping in dummy
CONSIDER THE ORDER
• Draw trumps first.
• Develop the extra heart tricks early.
• High card from the short side first.

♥A is driven out, declarer's high hearts should draw the defenders' hearts if they are divided 3-2. Declarer's remaining hearts will be winners. Before taking the diamond winners, declarer's strategy should be to draw the defenders' trumps so they can't trump a diamond winner.

Declarer can try to win the first trick with dummy's ♣K but that won't work because South holds the ♣A. If the defenders lead a second club, declarer can trump.

Declarer's next play is to lead a low heart to dummy's ♥Q, playing the high card from the short side first. This play accomplishes two things. It starts to promote winners in the heart suit and draws trumps at the same time.

If South wins the ♥A and leads another club, declarer can again win the trick with a trump. Now declarer draws the defenders' remaining trumps with the ♥K and ♥J. When the missing hearts prove to be divided 3-2, declarer's remaining hearts are winners.

Finally, it is safe to take the diamond winners and the ♠A. Declarer finishes with ten tricks: one spade, five hearts, and four diamonds. Game contract bid and made.

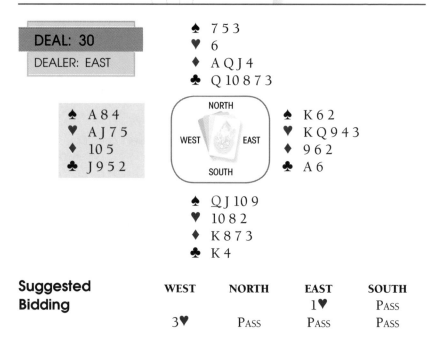

DEAL: 30

DEALER: EAST

NORTH

♠ 7 5 3
♥ 6
♦ A Q J 4
♣ Q 10 8 7 3

WEST

♠ A 8 4
♥ A J 7 5
♦ 10 5
♣ J 9 5 2

EAST

♠ K 6 2
♥ K Q 9 4 3
♦ 9 6 2
♣ A 6

SOUTH

♠ Q J 10 9
♥ 10 8 2
♦ K 8 7 3
♣ K 4

Suggested Bidding

WEST	NORTH	EAST	SOUTH
		1♥	PASS
3♥	PASS	PASS	PASS

East is the dealer and has 13 valuation points: 12 high-card points plus 1 length point. East opens 1♥, the five-card major suit.

South has 9 high-card points, not enough to enter the auction.

West has 10 high-card points and, with support for East's major, can add 1 dummy point for the doubleton diamond. To show the strength and support, West jumps to 3♥, inviting opener to continue to game with a little extra.

North has 9 high-card points plus 1 length point for the five-card suit. North doesn't have enough to come into the auction at this point and passes.

West's jump raise shows four-card support and 11-12 points. East has a minimum opening with nothing extra. East turns down the invitation by passing. South passes and the auction is over.

Suggested Opening Lead

South is on declarer's left and makes the opening lead. South leads the ♠Q, top of the solid sequence.

Declarer's Plan

West puts down the dummy and declarer makes a plan. East's goal is to take at least nine tricks. There are two sure tricks in spades, five in hearts, and one in clubs. One more trick is required.

East browses Declarer's Checklist. Declarer has more diamonds than dummy. This provides an opportunity to trump a diamond loser in the dummy.

In considering the order, declarer must be sure to leave at least one trump in the dummy.

> ┌─ **DECLARER'S PLAN—THE ABC'S** ─┐
>
> Declarer: East   Contract: 3♥
>
> **ASSESS THE SITUATION**
> | | |
> |---|---|
> | Goal | 9 |
> | Sure Tricks | 8 |
> | Extra Tricks Needed | 1 |
>
> **BROWSE DECLARER'S CHECKLIST**
> Promotion
> Length
> Finesse
> Trumping in dummy 1 in diamonds
>
> **CONSIDER THE ORDER**
> - Draw trumps first.
> - Keep a trump in dummy to ruff a diamond.
> - Develop the extra diamond trick early.

After winning the first spade trick, declarer can afford to draw the defenders' trumps. This takes three rounds when the missing hearts are divided 3-1[25]. Declarer still has a trump left in the dummy.

Next, declarer prepares to trump a diamond in the dummy by giving up a trick in the suit to the defenders. Suppose the defenders win and lead another spade. Declarer wins this trick and gives up a second diamond trick. Now dummy is void in diamonds.

The defenders can win the second diamond trick and take their established spade winner. Suppose they now lead a club. Declarer wins the ♣A and leads the last diamond, ruffing with dummy's last trump. The defenders eventually get a club trick, but that's all.

Declarer takes five heart tricks plus a diamond ruff in the dummy. Together with the two spade winners and club winner, that's nine tricks. East-West make the partscore contract.

---

[25] If the missing trumps were divided 4-0, declarer would have to switch to diamonds after a defender showed out on the first round. Declarer couldn't afford to continue drawing trumps.

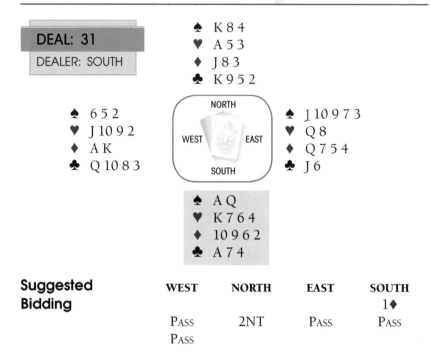

DEAL: 31

DEALER: SOUTH

NORTH
♠ K 8 4
♥ A 5 3
♦ J 8 3
♣ K 9 5 2

WEST
♠ 6 5 2
♥ J 10 9 2
♦ A K
♣ Q 10 8 3

EAST
♠ J 10 9 7 3
♥ Q 8
♦ Q 7 5 4
♣ J 6

SOUTH
♠ A Q
♥ K 7 6 4
♦ 10 9 6 2
♣ A 7 4

Suggested Bidding

WEST	NORTH	EAST	SOUTH
			1♦
PASS	2NT	PASS	PASS
PASS			

South is the dealer and values the hand as 13 points, all in high cards. With no five-card major, South opens 1♦, the longer minor.

West has 10 high-card points and passes.

North has 11 high-card points but doesn't have a four-card or longer major suit to show and doesn't have support for South's 1♦ opening. With a balanced hand, North can describe the strength by making an invitational jump to 2NT, showing 11-12 points.

East, with 6 high-card points and 1 length point, passes.

South doesn't have anything extra for the opening bid and settles for partscore by passing.

West passes and the auction is finished. North is declarer in a partscore contract of 2NT.

Suggested Opening Lead

East, on declarer's left, makes the opening lead. East leads the ♠J, top of the solid sequence in the suit.

Declarer's Plan

After East's opening lead, South puts down the dummy and declarer makes a plan. North's goal is to take eight tricks. There are three sure spade tricks, two hearts, and two clubs. One more trick is needed.

Declarer browses the checklist. It is possible that an extra trick could be developed through length in either hearts or clubs if the defenders' cards in either suit are divided 3-3.

DECLARER'S PLAN—THE ABC'S

Declarer: North   Contract: 2NT

ASSESS THE SITUATION

Goal	8
Sure Tricks	7
Extra Tricks Needed	1

BROWSE DECLARER'S CHECKLIST

Promotion	1 in diamonds
Length	
Finesse	
Trumping in dummy	

CONSIDER THE ORDER

- Develop the extra diamond trick early.

However, with six missing cards, the odds favor a 4-2 division. There is a surer method.

A trick can be developed in diamonds through promotion, even though declarer is missing the top three cards. Three tricks will have to be lost, but one trick will eventually be developed.

After winning the first spade trick, declarer immediately leads a diamond to drive out one of the defenders' winners in the suit. Suppose West wins and returns partner's suit, leading another spade. Declarer wins in dummy and leads another diamond, driving out another high diamond. Suppose West wins and leads another spade. Declarer wins the ♠K and leads diamonds for a third time, driving out the defender's last high diamond.

East wins the third diamond trick for the defense and can take the two established spade winners, but declarer has the rest of the tricks. Declarer takes three spade tricks, two hearts, one diamond, and two clubs, making the 2NT contract.

If declarer did not go after the diamond suit, the contract could be defeated. The defenders can establish winners in spades and the other suits and declarer will fall a trick short.

DEAL: 32	♠ K 8 5 3
DEALER: WEST	♥ A 8 4
	♦ 6
	♣ A J 8 6 5

♠ 10 6 2
♥ Q 10 7 3
♦ Q J 10 8
♣ K 4

NORTH
WEST — EAST
SOUTH

♠ 9
♥ K 9 5
♦ K 7 4 3 2
♣ Q 10 9 3

♠ A Q J 7 4
♥ J 6 2
♦ A 9 5
♣ 7 2

Suggested Bidding

WEST	NORTH	EAST	SOUTH
PASS	1♣	PASS	1♠
PASS	2♠	PASS	4♠
PASS	PASS	PASS	

West is the dealer and, with 8 high-card points, passes.

North has 12 high-card points plus 1 length point for the five-card suit, enough to open. North opens 1♣, the longest suit.

East, with 8 high-card points and 1 length point for the five-card suit, passes.

South, with 12 high-card points plus 1 length point for the five-card suit, responds 1♠.

West passes. North has four-card support for responder's major and can revalue the hand counting dummy points. There are 12 high-card points plus 3 dummy points for the singleton diamond. The total of 15 points still leaves the hand in the minimum-strength category so North raises to 2♠.

East passes. Having found a fit in spades, South has enough to take the partnership to the game level by jumping to 4♠.

West, North, and East pass, ending the auction.

Suggested Opening Lead

West, to declarer's left, makes the opening lead. West leads the ♦Q, top of the solid sequence in that suit.

Declarer's Plan

After West leads, the North hand comes down as the dummy and declarer makes a plan. South's goal is to take ten tricks.

South counts the sure tricks. There are five spade tricks, one heart, one diamond, and one club. Two more tricks are needed.

South browses Declarer's Checklist. Since there are more diamonds in South's hand than in the dummy, declarer can plan to trump two diamonds in the dummy. This will provide both the extra tricks required.

DECLARER'S PLAN—THE ABC'S

Declarer: South   Contract: 4♠

ASSESS THE SITUATION
Goal	10
Sure Tricks	8
Extra Tricks Needed	2

BROWSE DECLARER'S CHECKLIST
Promotion
Length
Finesse
Trumping in dummy   2 in diamonds

CONSIDER THE ORDER
- Keep trumps in dummy to ruff the diamonds.
- Develop the extra diamond tricks early.

In considering the order, declarer has to make sure that there are enough spades in dummy with which to trump the diamonds.

After winning the first diamond trick with the ♦A, declarer doesn't want to draw the trumps right away because there is work to be done in the diamond suit. It is convenient to immediately lead a diamond and trump in the dummy. Declarer can come back to the South hand with a spade winner to lead the last diamond and trump it in the dummy.

With this work done, declarer can draw the remaining trumps and take the ♥A and ♣A to make the contract. Declarer gets ten tricks: five spade winners in the South hand, the ♦A, two diamond ruffs in the dummy, the ♥A, and the ♣A. North-South get their game bonus.

Appendices

Appendix 1 – Mechanics

There are different ways to play bridge. Two of the most popular are:

Rubber or social bridge. This form of the game is used when there are only four players or there are several tables and the players want to change partners throughout the session. The length of social games is decided by the players.

Duplicate or tournament bridge. This is used in clubs and tournaments, usually with larger groups of players. The players remain in set partnerships throughout the session which lasts for a prearranged period of time, usually 2½ to 3½ hours.

Rubber Bridge

This form of the game is played with two decks of cards with different backs or designs. Unless the partnerships have been prearranged, one deck is shuffled and spread face down on the table. All four players select a card and turn it face up. The players with the two highest-ranking cards become one partnership and the players with the two lowest-ranking cards become the other partnership. If two cards of the same rank are drawn – two kings for example—the tie is broken by the rank of the suits: clubs being the lowest, then diamonds, hearts, and spades.

The player who drew the highest-ranking card becomes the initial dealer and has the choice of seats at the table. The dealer's partner sits opposite and the other pair arranges themselves on either side. The dealer has the choice of which deck of cards will be used for the first deal.

For example, suppose the ♥Q, ♦Q, ♣7, and ♠3 are drawn. The players drawing the ♥Q and ♦Q would be partners against the players who drew the ♣7 and ♠3. The player drawing the ♥Q would be the dealer since it outranks the ♦Q.

The cards to be dealt are shuffled by the opponent to the dealer's left. The shuffled deck is then passed to the opponent on the dealer's right who *cuts* the deck by taking approximately half the cards off the top of the deck and placing them in front of the dealer. The dealer completes the cut by taking the bottom half of the cards and placing them on top. The dealer then picks up the cards and deals them out one at a time in a clockwise direction, starting with the player to the dealer's left. While one deck of cards is being dealt, the partner of the dealer shuffles the other deck of cards and places it to the right.

At the end of play, the partnerships agree on the tricks won and lost and the result is scored by a member of each partnership (see Appendix 2).

After each deal has been played out, the position of dealer moves clockwise around the table. The previously shuffled second deck will be on the new dealer's left. It is passed across to the opponent on the dealer's right, cut, and the new deal commences. The cards from the previous deal are gathered by the dealer's partner, shuffled, and placed on the right ready for the next deal.

Play continues until the rubber is complete (see Appendix 2). At that point, new partnerships can be selected and a new rubber begins. If the players prefer, the partnerships can be rearranged so that everyone plays with the other three players at the table.

Duplicate Bridge

In this format, the partnerships are usually prearranged and each pair is assigned to a table in either the North-South or East-West direction. The directions are indicated by a *guide card* on each table. The partnership can agree which player sits in which direction but must then remain in that direction throughout the game. The North-South pairs usually stay at their pre-assigned table throughout the game. The East-West pairs move from table to table after playing a *round*, a preset number of deals.

The cards are dealt only once at the beginning of the game and the four hands are placed in the pockets of a *duplicate board*. The deal will remain intact throughout the game.

The board is placed on the table so that the compass directions marked on the board match the guide card on the table. The four players each take the hand out of the appropriate pocket. The dealer and vulnerability (see Appendix 2) are pre-assigned on each board.

The player in the assigned dealer's position begins the auction and the bidding proceeds as in other forms of the game, although *bidding boxes* are commonly used in place of spoken bids.

When the auction is complete and the contract and declarer have been decided, the player to the declarer's left makes the opening lead. It is common practice in duplicate bridge for the opening lead to be made face down. This prevents any penalty if the lead was inadvertently made by the wrong player. Once everyone is satisfied, the lead can be turned face up.

At the end of play, the partnerships agree on the tricks won or lost and the result is scored (see Appendix 2). The cards in front of each player are then picked up and placed in the appropriate pocket of the duplicate board so the same deal can be played at other tables.

Appendix 2 – Scoring

A partnership scores *points* in three ways:

- Trick Score for bidding and making contracts.
- Bonus Points (see below).
- Penalty Points for defeating the opponents' contract.

These points should not be confused with the valuation points used to estimate the trick-taking potential of a hand.

Trick Score

The partnership that wins the auction scores points for making the contract depending on the strain:

- 20 points per trick bid and made in clubs or diamonds, the minor suits.
- 30 points per trick bid and made in hearts or spades, the major suits.
- 40 points for the first trick and 30 points for each subsequent trick in notrump.

The trick score applies only to tricks taken beyond the initial six tricks (book) assumed in the contract. A contract of Two Spades (2♠) is a commitment to take eight tricks (6 + 2 = 8). If declarer makes eight tricks, the partnership gets a trick score of 60 points (30 + 30). A contract of 3NT would be worth a trick score of 100 points (40 + 30 + 30).

Game is a total trick score of 100 or more points. A game can be scored in a single deal by bidding and making the following contracts:

GAME CONTRACTS		
Game in Notrump	3NT (nine tricks)	40 + 30 + 30 = 100
Game in a Major	4♥ or 4♠ (ten tricks)	30 + 30 + 30 + 30 = 120
Game in a Minor	5♣ or 5♦ (eleven tricks)	20 + 20 + 20 + 20 + 20 = 100

A contract that is worth less than 100 points is called a *partscore*. For example, a contract of 2NT is worth only 70 points (40 + 30); a contract of 4♦ is worth 80 points (20 + 20 + 20 + 20).

Bonuses

Some bonuses are awarded depending on the format of the game.

RUBBER BRIDGE

The objective in rubber bridge is to be the first partnership to make two games of 100 or more points – a *rubber* is the best two out of three. In rubber bridge, a game can be scored in a single deal or by making two or more partscores that add up to 100 points.

When a partnership makes a game, it becomes *vulnerable* and a new game begins. Any partscore the other side has no longer counts toward the next game. When a vulnerable partnership makes its second game, it wins the rubber and receives a *rubber bonus*:

- 500 if the partnership won the rubber two games to one.
- 700 if the partnership won the rubber two games to none.

In rubber bridge, an *honors bonus* of 100 points is awarded if a player holds four of the honors in the trump suit and a bonus of 150 points if a player holds all five honors in the trump suit or all four aces in a notrump contract.

The points scored are recorded on a score sheet that looks like this:

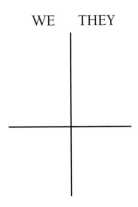

WE   THEY

Points won by your side are entered in the "WE" column; points won by the opponents are entered in the "THEY" column. The horizontal line is called *the line*. Trick scores for contracts bid and made go below the line; bonuses go above the line.

DUPLICATE BRIDGE

In duplicate bridge, each deal is scored separately. There is no carryover from one deal to the next. The vulnerability is pre-assigned on each board and bonuses for bidding and making contracts are awarded as follows:

- 300 for bidding and making a non vulnerable game contract.
- 500 for bidding and making a vulnerable game contract.
- 50 for bidding and making a partscore contract.

There are no bonuses for honors in duplicate scoring.

Slam Bonuses

The bonuses for bidding and making a small slam contract—12 tricks—and a grand slam—all 13 tricks—are the same in all forms of the game:

- 500 for a non vulnerable small slam.
- 750 for a vulnerable small slam.
- 1,000 for a non vulnerable grand slam.
- 1,500 for a vulnerable grand slam.

The slam bonus is in addition to the trick score and any rubber or game bonus.

Overtricks

If declarer makes more tricks than required for the contract, the trick score for each trick is added to the score (above the line in rubber bridge).

Penalty Points

If declarer doesn't make the required number of tricks, the opponents receive points for each *undertrick*:

- 50 points per undertrick when non vulnerable.
- 100 points per undertrick when vulnerable.

The size of the penalty can be increased if the contract is doubled or redoubled, but that is outside the scope of this book.

An Example of Rubber Bridge Scoring

Here is a sample rubber bridge score, with an explanation below for each numbered item.

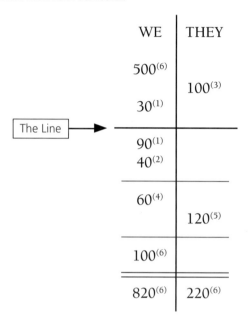

WE	THEY
500[6]	
	100[3]
30[1]	
The Line	
90[1]	
40[2]	
60[4]	
	120[5]
100[6]	
820[6]	220[6]

1) On the first deal, your side bids to a contract of 3♥ and makes the contract with an overtrick. You get a trick score of 90 (3 x 30) below the line and a score of 30 for the overtrick above the line. The overtrick doesn't count toward the game bonus.

2) On the second deal, you bid to a contract of 1NT and make exactly seven tricks. You get a trick score of 40 below the line. Since you now have a total of more than 100 points below the line, you win the first game. A line is drawn across the scoresheet to indicate that the first game is over. Your side is now vulnerable.

3) On the third deal, you bid to a contract of 2♦ and are defeated by one trick. Since you are vulnerable, the opponents get a penalty score of 100 points on their side, above the line.

4) On the fourth deal, you bid to a contract of 2♠ and make eight tricks. You get a trick score of 60 (2 x 30) below the line.

5) On the fifth deal, the opponents bid to a contract of 4♥ and make ten tricks. They receive 120 (4 x 30) points below the line. This is enough for a game and a second line is drawn across the scoresheet. Both sides are now vulnerable. Your previous partscore of 60 points is *cut off*—a fresh game begins.

6) On the sixth deal, your side bids to a contract of 3NT and makes nine tricks. You receive a trick score of 100 points (40 + 30 + 30) below the line. This is enough for your second game. You win the rubber two games to one and get a bonus of 500 points above the line. A double line is drawn across the sheet to indicate that the rubber is over and the scores for both sides are totaled. Your side scored 820 points; their side scored 220 points. Your side wins by a net of 600 points (820 – 220). On to the next rubber...

Appendix 3 – The Bidding Song

The following song (to the tune of *Row, Row, Row Your Boat*) can be a helpful reminder when making the opening bid:

> *Bid, bid, bid your hand,*
> *But alas, alas,*
> *If you have fewer than 13 points,*
> *I guess you'll have to pass.*

> *Bid, bid, bid your cards,*
> *With a balanced hand.*
> *If you have a three-point range (15–17)*
> *One notrump's your stand.*

> *Bid, bid, bid your hand,*
> *You don't need charades,*
> *But you'll need a five-card suit*
> *To start with hearts or spades.*

> *Bid, bid, bid your cards,*
> *Don't sit around and stew,*
> *Open your longer minor suit*
> *With nothing else to do.*

Glossary

Attitude Signal—A defensive carding signal to let partner know whether you want a particular suit led. A high card is an encouraging signal; a low card is a discouraging signal. (page 54)

Auction—The process of determining the contract through a series of bids. (page 5)

Auction Bridge—An early form of the game that introduced bidding to determine the strain of the contract. (page 5)

Balanced Hand—A hand with no voids, no singletons, and no more than one doubleton. (page 38)

Bid—An undertaking to win at least a specified number of tricks in a specified strain. (page 5)

Bidding—The various bids which make up the auction. (page 5)

Bidding Box—A device with the bids displayed on cards to allow the auction to be conducted silently. (page 187)

Bidding Ladder—The order in which bids can be made, starting with 1♣ and ending with 7NT. (page 6)

Bidding Message—Whether a bid is forcing, invitational or signoff. (page 48)

Bonus—Points scored for making a partscore, game, or slam or for defeating the opponents' contract. (page 9, 188)

Book—The first six tricks taken by declarer. (page 5)

Broken Sequence—A sequence of cards in a suit where the third card from the top is missing but not the next lower-ranking card(s). For example, ♥K-Q-10-9, ♦J-10-8. (page 17)

Call—Any bid, double, redouble or pass. (page 5)

Competition—An auction in which both sides are bidding to try and win the contract. (page 6)

Combined Hands—Both hands belonging to one partnership. (page 12)

Contract—The undertaking by declarer's side to win at least a specific number of tricks in a specific strain as determined by the final bid in the auction. (page 8)

Contract Bridge—The modern form of the game which awards bonuses for bidding and making contracts. (page 8)

Convention—A bid which conveys a meaning other than what would normally be attributed to it. (page 43)

Cut (the Cards)—To draw a random card from a face down pack of cards; to divide the deck into approximately two equal halves and place the bottom half on the top. (page 186)

Cut Off—If the opponents have a partscore when a non vulnerable game is made in rubber bridge, the partscore is cut off and doesn't count toward the next game. (page 193)

Deal—The distribution of the cards to the four players. (page 1)

Dealer—The player who distributes the cards, face-down, starting with the player on the left. The dealer has the first opportunity to open the bidding or to pass. (page 1)

Deck—The fifty-two cards used in a game of bridge. It contains four suits, with thirteen cards in each suit. (page 1)

Declarer—The player from the side that won the auction, who first bid the strain named in the contract. (page 7)

Defeat—Stop declarer from making a contract. (page 8)

Defense—The side that did not win the auction. (page 8)

Discard—Play a card to a trick which is from a different suit than the one led and is not a trump. (page 2)

Distribution—The number of cards held in each suit by a particular player; the number of cards held in a particular suit by the partnership. (page 11)

Double—A call that increases the bonus for making or defeating a contract. It can also be used to ask partner to bid a suit.(page 5)

Doubleton—A holding of two cards in a suit. (page 38)

Draw Trump—Playing the trump suit until the opponents have none left. (page 16)

Dummy—The hand of declarer's partner that is placed face up on the table after the opening lead. (page 7)

Dummy Points—Points used in place of length points when valuing a hand in support of partner's suit: void, 5 points; singleton, 3 points; doubleton, 1 point. (page 77)

Establish—Set up sure tricks by driving out winning cards in the opponents' hands. (page 15)

Finesse—A method of building extra tricks by trapping an opponent's high card(s). (page 49, 129)

Five-Card Major (Style)—The partnership agreement that an opening bid of 1♥ or 1♠ promises five or more cards in the suit. (page 74)

Follow Suit—Play a card in the suit led. (page 2)

Forcing (Bid)—A bid partner is not expected to pass. (page 48)

Fourth Highest—A lead of the fourth card down from the top in a suit. (page 17)

Game—A total trick score of 100 or more points. (page 9, 189)

Game Contract—A contract which has a trick score value of 100 or more points. (page 9, 189)

Grand Slam—A contract to take all thirteen tricks. (page 9)

Guide Card—A printed card placed on the table that indicates the player directions and instructions for the movement in duplicate games. (page 187)

Hand—The cards held by one player. Sometimes used to refer to the full deal of all four hands. (page 1)

Hand Valuation—The method to determine the value of a particular hand during the auction. Usually a combination of high card strength and suit length or shortness. (page 10)

HCPs—An abbreviation for high-card points. (page 10)

High Card—One of the top four cards in a suit: ace, king, queen, or jack. (page 10)

High Card Points—The value of high cards in a hand: ace, 4; king, 3; queen, 2; jack, 1. (page 10)

Higher-Ranking Suit—A suit that ranks higher on the Bidding Ladder than another suit. Spades are ranked highest; hearts are second; diamonds are third; clubs are the lowest-ranking suit. (page 6)

Honor (Card)—An ace, king, queen, jack or ten. (page 17)

Honors Bonus—A bonus score awarded in rubber bridge for holding four or more honors in the trump suit, or all four aces in a notrump contract. (page 190)

How High—The level at which the contract should be played. (page 40)

Interior Sequence—A holding in a suit that contains a sequence and a higher-ranking card that is not part of the sequence. For example, ♥A-J-10-9, ♦Q-10-9-8. (page 17)

Invitational—A bid which encourages partner to continue bidding while allowing partner to pass. (page 48)

Language of Bidding—The exchange of information during the auction through bids consisting of a number and a strain. (page 5)

Lead—The first card played to a trick (page 2)

Length Points—The valuation assigned to long suits in a hand: five-card suit, 1 point; six-card suit, 2 points; seven-card suit, 3 points; eight-card suit, 4 points. (page 11)

Level—The number of tricks the partnership contracts to take when it makes a bid. It includes an assumed six tricks (see Book). (page 5)

Line—The horizontal line on a rubber bridge scoresheet that divides the bonuses from the trick scores. (page 190)

Long(est) Suit—The suit with the most cards in a player's hand. (page 12)

Loser—A trick which might be lost to the opponents. (page 15)

Lower-Ranking Suit—A suit which is lower on the Bidding Ladder than another suit. (page 6)

Major (Suit) —Spades or hearts. (page 9, 42)

Make (A Contract)—Succeed in taking enough tricks to fulfill the contract. (page 8)

Minor (Suit)—Diamonds or clubs. (page 9, 42)

New Suit—A suit which has not previously been bid in the auction. (page 78)

Notrump—A contract with no trump suit. The highest card played in the suit led wins the trick. (page 4)

Offense—The partnership which wins the auction. (page 8)

One Level—The lowest level at which the auction can start. It represents seven tricks. (page 5)

Open the Bidding—Make the first bid in the auction. (page 5)

Opener's Rebid—The opening bidder's second bid. (page 47)

Opening Bid—The first bid made during an auction. (page 12)

Opening Lead—The card led to the first trick. The player to declarer's left leads first. (page 7)

Overcall—A bid made after the opponents have opened the bidding. (page 6)

Overtrick—A trick won by declarer in excess of the number required to make the contract. (page 10)

Partnership—The two players seated opposite each other at the table. (page 1)

Part Game—See partscore. (page 9)

Partscore—A contract that does not receive a game bonus if made. (page 9, 189)

Pass—A call specifying that a player does not want to bid at that turn. (page 5)

Pattern—The number of cards held in each suit in a player's hand. (page 38)

Penalty—The bonus awarded to the defenders for defeating a contract. (page 191)

Points—Points are awarded on a score sheet for bidding and making contracts and for defeating the opponents' contracts. (page 188)

Point Count—A method of hand valuation, which assigns points for high cards held and for distribution. (page 10)

Promotion—Developing one or more cards into winners by driving out any higher-ranking cards held by the opponents. (page 50)

Rank of Cards—The cards in each suit are ranked in order during the play: the ace is the highest, then the king, queen, jack, ten ... down to the two. (page 1)

Rank of the Suits—The suits are ranked in order during the bidding: spades are highest, then hearts, diamonds and clubs. Notrump ranks higher than spades. (page 6)

Raise—Supporting partner's suit by bidding the suit at a higher level. (page 76)

Rebid—A second bid by opener or responder. (page 47)

Redouble—A call that increases the bonuses for making or defeating a contract that has already been doubled. (page 5)

Respond—Make a bid, other than pass, when partner has previously made a bid. (page 13)

Responder—The partner of the opening bidder. (page 13)

Responder's Rebid—Responder's second bid. (page 89)

Round—A specified number of deals during a duplicate bridge session during which the players remain at the same table. (page 187)

Rubber—The unit of play in rubber bridge which ends when one partnership wins two games. (page 178)

Rubber Bonus—The bonus awarded for winning the rubber when playing rubber bridge. (page 189)

Rubber Bridge—One of the popular forms of contract bridge. (page 3, 185)

Ruff(ing)—Play a trump to a trick when holding no cards in the suit led. Same as trumping. (page 4)

Second Hand—The hand playing the second card to a trick. (page 19)

Sequence—Three or more consecutive cards in a suit. (page 17)

Set—Defeat the contract. (page 8)

Shape—The number of cards held in each suit in a player's hand. (page 11)

Short Side—The partnership hand with fewer cards in a specific suit. (page 53)

Showing Support—Agreeing with partner's suggested trump suit by raising the suit to a higher level. (page 75)

Signoff (Bid) —A bid that asks partner to pass. (page 48)

Singleton—A holding of one card in a suit. (page 38)

Slam—A contract to take twelve or thirteen tricks. (page 9)

Small Slam—A contract to take twelve tricks. (page 9)

Stayman Convention—An artificial response of 2♣ to an opening bid of 1NT, asking opener to bid a four-card or longer major suit. (page 43)

Strain—The suit, or notrump, specified in a bid. (page 5)

Strength—The point count value of a hand. (page 11)

Suits—The four groups of cards in the deck, each having a characteristic symbol: spades (♠), hearts (♥), diamonds (♦), and clubs (♣). (page 1)

Support—The number of cards held in a suit that partner has bid. (page 75)

Sure Trick—A trick which can be taken without giving up the lead to the opponents. (page 15)

Third Hand—The hand playing the third card to a trick. (page 19)

Trick—The four cards contributed during each round of the play. Starting with the player on lead, each player contributes a card in clockwise rotation. In notrump, the highest-ranking card played in the suit led wins the tricks. In a suit contract, a trump played to a trick automatically wins unless a higher trump is played. The player winning a trick leads to the next trick. (page 2)

Trick Score—The points scored for contracts bid and made. (page 188)

Trump Fit—A combined partnership holding of (ideally) eight or more cards in a suit. (page 7)

Trump Suit—The suit, if any, named in the contract. (page 4)

Trumping—Playing a trump on a trick when void in the suit led. (page 4)

Two-Over-One—A non-jump response in a new suit at the two level after an opening one-level bid in a suit. (page 78)

Unbalanced Hand—A hand with a void, a singleton, or more than one doubleton. (page 38)

Undertrick—Each trick by which declarer's side fails to fulfill the contract. (page 10, 191)

Up the Line—Bidding the cheapest of two or more four-card suits (page 114)

Valuation (Points)—A method of estimating the value of a hand during the auction, usually a combination of values for high cards and length. (page 10)

Void—A holding of zero cards in a suit. (page 38)

Vulnerability—The status of the deal during a round of bridge which affects the size of the bonuses awarded for making or defeating contracts. Bonuses and penalties are higher when declarer's side is vulnerable. (page 189)

Where—The strain in which the contract should be played. (page 40)

Winner—A card held by one of the players that will win a trick when it is played. (page 15)